PRAISE FOR ALAN CHEUSE'S

A Trance After Breakfast

"It's very good to travel with Cheuse, the literate Jersey boy who's lived long enough to think it's time to see the rest of the world. As our guide, he's seeing it all for the first time, just like we are (though he's read about it), so that he's dazzled, moved, impressed, shocked, instructed and provoked. He is us, in other words. And he relishes the vast world outside his ken as if it were a rare jewel."

—Richard Ford

"Alan Cheuse's evocations of place—the water world of his youth on the Jersey shore, his tramps in Bali and New Zealand, his inquiries on California's border with Mexico—are Whitmanesque in their enthusiasm and captivating in all their particulars. His observations on the way various writers have approached Southeast Asian settings in their novels, on the one hand, and his thoughts on Jewish cultural life in Mexico, on the other, are the reflections of a charming and original mind."

—Barry Lopez

"Serious readers have come to think they know Alan Cheuse's voice. His is the discerning baritone on NPR. But he possesses a range of voices that covers the spectrum—comic, declarative, elegiac, lyrical, compassionate—and all of them are on marvelous display in *A Trance After Breakfast*. More than just a collection of travel essays, the book describes vivid inner and outer journeys, and captures with special poignancy the ambivalences of borderlands. The three pieces about San Diego's shadow city, Tijuana, are worth the price of a plane ticket anywhere on earth."

—Michael Mewshaw

"This is how I want to learn to travel, with Alan Cheuse's eye and ear and brain and, most of all, heart. 'A love affair of fierce currents,' indeed. *A Trance After Breakfast* will endure as a model for the engaged explorer, even the armchair sort."

—Josephine Humphreys

"More than a century ago, as Native American cultures were struggling to survive, the American photographer Edward Curtis was recording the native people in full regalia on the striking lands where their people had lived for centuries. *To Catch the Lightning* tells Curtis's story vividly and eloquently. It is a great American story, about a life spent preserving and honoring those elements of life which are most respected and beloved. Alan Cheuse is to be congratulated for this vivid novel."

—William Kittredge, author of
The Willow Field and *The Next Rodeo*

"The photography and cinema of Edward Curtis exist at the intersection of art, history, anthropology, and technology. He was an essentially American kind of genius, and Alan Cheuse has transformed his life into compelling fiction that digs deep into the mystery and sacrifice and selfishness of creative vision."

—Charles Frazier, author of
Cold Mountain and *Thirteen Moons*

"Bravo to Cheuse for this incarnation of a major and unfairly forgotten American artist, capturing an era so crucial in Native American, and therefore, American history. I found it immediate and innovative."

—Diane Johnson, author of
Le Divorce and *Lulu in Marrakech*

A TRANCE AFTER BREAKFAST

AND OTHER PASSAGES

ALAN CHEUSE

SOURCEBOOKS, INC.®
NAPERVILLE, ILLINOIS

Published by Sourcebooks, Inc.
P.O. Box 4410, Naperville, Illinois 60567-4410
(630) 961-3900
Fax: (630) 961-2168
www.sourcebooks.com

Library of Congress Cataloging-in-Publication Data

Cheuse, Alan.
  A trance after breakfast : and other passages / by Alan Cheuse.
    p. cm.
  1. Voyages and travels. 2. Cheuse, Alan—Travel. I. Title.
G465.C394 2009
910.4092—dc22
                        2009008769

Printed and bound in the United States of America.
VP 10 9 8 7 6 5 4 3 2 1

For Kris, fellow traveler

CONTENTS

ACKNOWLEDGMENTS

With thanks to Shana Drehs, Ruth Reichl, Jocelyn Zuckerman, Robert Fogarty, Robert Wilson, Jim Holman, and, in memory, Judith Moore.

INTRODUCTION: TRAVELING IN PLACE

There's something to be said for staying in one place over a long period of time. I just don't know what that is. Our most ancient ancestors, who presumably huddled nightly in caves or set up encampments along freshly flowing streams, had to be on the move or die. They followed the food, they followed the seasons. It wasn't until that second wave of advanced thinking that brought them from the hunting to the gathering phase that they found it valuable to stay in one place.

But did they want to, or did they find it merely convenient because of the crops that came in?

I guess it's the old hunter mind in my modern head that keeps me going, that makes for the nomadic urge that takes me over every fall and, as it has every year for the past thirty years, by early summer sends me out to California. (In fact, I've begun making these notes while traveling a couple hundred miles an hour at thirty-four thousand feet, on the way west again, gaining in an afternoon what our nineteenth-century forebears would take months and months to gain on the overland routes to Oregon and California.) Autumn in the east is lovely. But after the leaves fall, I begin to find something arising in me that needs consoling, that the place where I live most of the year cannot supply. For a while love and family and writing and reading and teaching give me enough back from what I give to them that I can function at a pretty good level without moping. But by the beginning of December, with its bare trees, chilly temperatures, and the prospect, or, worse, the arrival of disruptive snows, I slide into a worse funk, one that, alas, alas, even love can't fully obliterate.

Our oldest parents, those cave huddlers, knew the reasons why. The sun was going out, they surmised, and so were the stars. They built bonfires and sent the smoke trailing upward into the heavens, to reignite the failing lights in the sky for another season, eventually bringing spring around again. For the majority of post-pagan folk this belief in homiletic magic became codified as Christmas, and all the religious mental and spiritual paraphernalia attached to it. New pagans from New Jersey, such as yours truly, who grew up unaffected—sorry, old folks—by any religion, though Judaism afflicted some of us, Catholicism and Methodism, others, had to find ways to get through the dull cold ache of winter—and the boring heat of summer, not to mention the dying season of autumn and a pathetic Jersey spring.

Even as children our urge to wander saved us, or at least, seemed to satisfy the ache in our souls. As soon as we could toddle, we tried to walk out of the house. As soon as we could navigate, we walked around the block. As soon as we knew how to cross the street without getting hit by a car, we hurried down to the beach where the Raritan River ran into the bay, and we raced along the water's edge. As soon as we had a nickel, we walked to the ferry slip a few blocks north and east and crossed the Arthur Kill to the lower tip of Staten Island.

Sit still!

Mother constantly gave that command. Teachers did, too.

But we were always fidgeting, at the least, while sitting at the dinner table or at a school desk. Fidgeting, the physiological effect of boredom, was the way we traveled in place. Fidgeting was traveling that took you nowhere.

Only when we began to read in earnest did we discover a form of mental travel. Our fidgeting stopped. First it was the

Captain Horatio Hornblower novels that stopped it. I read those, I traveled on the high seas, sailed into combat on the open ocean. And then science fiction stopped me from fidgeting. I blasted off to other planets, sailed on solar winds, passed through a number of wormholes into other parts of the universe, and from time to time went from Time to Time.

Mars was Heaven until long years later, at the university, I read Dante and discovered a fuller and more mature, if less exciting, Paradise. I began to notice the distinction between life and art—life was moving around from place to place while art was traveling.

So there is travel and there is travel. Or as Hemingway put it in his introduction to the second edition of *For Whom the Bell Tolls*, there is a distinction between motion and action. Motion, whether skiing (which is what he was referring to) or any other variety of moving around, is one thing. Action, which is motion with a purpose beyond the merely literal, trumps mere motion. Sex without love (to use a title of a marvelous poem by Sharon Olds)—that's *motion*. Sex with someone you love—that's *action*.

In this respect, most narrative art tells an action story about traveling, whether literal or metaphorical or symbolic, and the best narratives fuse the two realms.

Our greatest heroes have always been travelers. Go back and read the oldest narratives we have in the West, from the epic of *Gilgamesh* to *The Iliad* and *The Odyssey*, and you'll see that this is so.

Gilgamesh, king of Uruk, sick from grief after the death of his beloved half-animal, half-human friend Enkidu, sets out from his city on a journey that takes him across oceans and down into their depths, where he fetches up the mysterious *moly* plant that will bestow eternal life on whomever can keep it.

King Agamemnon and his Greek warriors, the great Achilles foremost among them, cross an ocean to fight the war against Troy.

Odysseus, over the course of ten years, heads home from the war, wandering among Mediterranean islands and having fabulous adventures before returning at last to Ithaka.

Aeneas travels a similar route, from east to west, and makes landfall on the Italian coast.

Chaucer's pilgrims ride from London to Canterbury.

From a village in La Mancha whose name I do not care to remember, Don Quixote and his sidekick, Sancho Panza, set out on their journey.

All great narrative literature takes us on journeys, from the beginning of our time to the present day.

But wait, wait! I know. You're saying Proust's great alter ego, the narrator Marcel of *Remembrance of Things Past*, doesn't get out much. In fact, though he stays in his room in the early volumes of that extraordinary novel, he travels mentally, in his imagination, back into the days he believed he had lost forever.

I don't rest my case; who wants to rest? But this does take us to the point where we have to admit that life is overland travel, the literal kind, and art is jet travel, powered by the imagination and leaving metaphoric truths like contrails in the sky as it moves along.

This notion of metaphor, which you might call jet-powered language, my fellow pilgrims, is an important one when it comes to any kind of writing, travel narrative or not. Without metaphor, a piece of writing tends to seem raw, to use Claude Levi-Strauss's great distinction, rather than cooked. When it comes to travel writing, which I see as a form of the personal essay, or perhaps I should say the personal essay on the road, the merely literal piece is something we need for logistical purposes—as in the listing in Frommer's guides or Lonely Planet guides—but a travel piece, whether an essay or a full-length book, that rises to the level of the metaphorical, which is to say, the symbolic, becomes a journey that has more meaning than a simple trip. It becomes a journey recollected by the writer that the writer then turns into a journey for the reader to remember.

When Andrew Harvey travels to a Buddhist monastery in Ladakh or Bruce Chatwin takes us to the Australian outback or to Patagonia, we begin with travel to a foreign, often exotic place, but that, as the literal location always is, is only the beginning. Because along with some extra shirts and underwear, we always bring with us that which is usually impossible to leave behind at home, which is to say, ourselves, our spirits, our, if you will, souls.

By definition then, the best travel writing carries us along on a soul-journey, the sort of trip that may or may not tell you about the best hotels and the good places to eat but certainly, if it lives up to this standard, dramatizes how the heart learns about itself in relation to the world, making the foreign familiar and the familiar slightly foreign. Rather a broad definition, you may say. And I have to confess, yes, this definition embraces just about any serious variety of narrative, personal history, social history, character study, or study of the land and landscape (I'm thinking here of the first half of the great, mostly unsung masterpiece of Brazilian literature by Euclides da Cunha, *Rebellion in the Backlands,* in which the author spends many, many pages describing the terrain of northeast Brazil before narrating the story of the insurrection of a religious sect against the federal government that took place in that part of the country). All of these are varieties of narrative you might not think of at first as travel writing.

This accounting implies, and rightly so, I believe, that all of these varieties of narrative—personal essay, dramatic anecdote, personal history, social history, national history, character study, nature writing—inform good travel writing.

That's why some of our best travel writers—and here I'm thinking of the late Bruce Chatwin, and the very much alive Paul Theroux, and a host of others including Herbert Gold, Mary Morris, Ana Menendez, Francisco Goldman, and Kiran Desai—are also some of our best fiction writers. Good fiction always pushes off from the literal and ascends immediately above it or beyond it.

As the twentieth-century literary critic Kenneth Burke used to say, man is the symbol-making animal. When warrior ants travel, they make bridges of their own bodies so that the rest of the army can cross a stream. When spiders travel, they make webs to secure their nourishment. When human beings travel, if you accept Burke's straightforward pronouncement about us as a species, we make symbols. We turn the literal stuff of our wanderings into something that doesn't seem visible but that we can feel the presence of nonetheless.

Put it this way. When I traveled to Bali I felt toward the land and the sky above it something akin to reverence and awe, for me a quite unexpected outcome. When I traveled to New Zealand's South Island, I encountered deep fjords and glaciers that took me out of myself and brought me back a slightly different person. When I go to Dublin—a place I confess I've never been but would love to lay my eyes on—and stand before the street sign for number 7 Eccles Street, I will be seeing far beyond the literal, all the way back to my first encounter with James Joyce's *Ulysses*, that great novel about an advertising salesman who lives at that address, with his wife, Molly.

Infusing a travel piece with soul is no more difficult than writing a good short story, which is to say it is quite difficult. But travel writing worth its salt is not complete without rising to the level of good, serious writing. Literal travel, travel without some empathetic engagement between the traveler and the destination, the location where the wanderer settles for a while, whether a few days or a week or month or year or lifetime, lacks some of that same heart and soul.

That's not an extravagant claim. Most readers can tell the difference between a practical piece from a guidebook or a newspaper travel section and something with more soul and heart. Most serious readers turn to travel literature for something other than a tip about the best hotel or restaurant. Just as travel—read "life"—is not complete for the writer until he or she writes about it, for many readers life and traveling are not complete without reading about it.

Perhaps travel writing and reading about travel are congenital.

My own father's life was clearly a journey, since in the mid-1930s as a young officer in the Red Air Force he had flown across the broad girth of Russia, and then, after a series of misadventures found himself on a ship to Japan and then in China; and then he made a passage to the United States, by way of Hawaii, and then took a train across America to New York. That seemed to be enough of a journey for him. He remained in our town of Perth Amboy, New Jersey (except for one trip back to Russia and another to Europe and Israel in the seventies and eighties), pretty much in place for the rest of his life.

At his funeral someone recited the last lines from the chapter near the end of *Ulysses* in which Leopold Bloom retires to his bed after a long day's wandering through Dublin: "He rests. He is weary. He has traveled."

That someone was me.

And I dedicate these travel pieces, long and short, most of which I wrote for various magazines, to his restless youth. Whether you read them while sitting in place or on an airplane or on a train or on shipboard, I hope you will find them invigorating (or, as my father used to say in his Russian-accented English, "inwigorating") and spirited and, with a little luck on my part, something resembling something soulful.

Tickets, please! All aboard!

HOME PLACES

AN ELBOW OF LAND

ater is best, the antique Greek poet Pindar announced in the opening of one of his great odes. And growing up in Perth Amboy, New Jersey, it was clear to me, and to a lot of my pals, that water made all the difference. Without the water, Perth Amboy would have been only one of a number of light-industrial northeastern towns where for a century or more immigrants were attracted by the possibility of work.

Water attracted the first inhabitants of the place, nomadic groups of Lenni Lenape Indians who drifted east off the main north-south trail that stretched from the Shrewsbury River to Minisink Island in the Delaware River and walked to the land's east edge, where the creeks ran into the bay, fishing for the clams so plentiful in these waters. The Indians were the first human beings to stop here, bested only in time by those catchers'-mitts-on-legs, the ancient horseshoe crabs which for millions of years had crawled up onto the beach to spawn.

Water drew the Swedish crews who sailed into the bay in the early 1600s and made their settlements to the west on both sides of the Delaware River. And water drew after them the Dutch sailors and traders who settled on the island of Manhattan and explored the upper reaches of the Hudson River and the lower estuaries of New York Harbor.

Approach our town by car and you immediately notice the particular relation of water and land. Forty-two thousand people, a large minority of them Spanish-speaking now, some blacks, a number of Italian Americans, many Catholics of Eastern European descent, and a dwindling minority of Jews and Protestants inhabit an elbow of land—the old Lenni Lenape word for the place was "ompoge," for "elbow" or point of land—that pokes out in a southwesterly direction into Raritan Bay just where the Raritan River, on the town's southern border, empties into that larger body of water. On the east runs the Arthur Kill, a mile-wide channel separating New Jersey from Staten Island, the New York City borough of Richmond.

Just say a few of those words over again—such as "Ompoge," which eventually became the name "Amboy," and Kill, which was originally the Dutch word "kull," meaning "creek," and read the signs on Smith Street, the town's main business street that runs east to west up from the old ferry slip at the Kill, signs for joyerías and bodegas and panicerías—and you have some idea of the historical, linguistic, and ethnic mix that is Perth Amboy, New Jersey.

There was a time, in the forties and fifties, when there was little Spanish in the air, but a lot of Polish and Hungarian and Rumanian. In those days my grandparents' accented English, studded with plentiful phrases in Yiddish, must have struck the ears of their Protestant neighbors as colorful and full of flavor, and a bit mysterious, too, and perhaps even threatening. Melting pot, mixing bowl, such traditional phrases come to mind when I think of the many national groups and linguistic clusters who made my hometown their home, too. A melting pot, yes—but a melting pot bounded on two sides by water.

A lay historian of Perth Amboy's past, a newsman named Harold E. Pickersgill, pointed out in a 1938 pamphlet that it wasn't until well past the middle of the seventeenth century, nearly fifty years after the first Europeans had trod here, that the English, to whom we usually attribute all historical power in New Jersey, began to play a role.

But when they did it was a large one. With the restoration of the House of Stuart bringing peace to the English, Charles II in 1664 gave to his brother, James, Duke of York, a huge tract of land that included what is now New Jersey, New York, and much of New England. (That same year a squadron of British warships arrived in New York Harbor to hurry along the Dutch withdrawal from the New World.) And around this time, as Pickersgill writes, the Duke of York transferred to Lord Berkeley and Sir George Carteret the large parcel of land originally called Nova Caesaria or New Jersey, the name deriving from Carteret's association with the defense of the Isle of Jersey or, as it was once known, Caesaria.

It wasn't long before Berkeley and Carteret divided their interests, with one governing West Jersey and the other East Jersey. Perth Amboy served as the capital of the East Jersey colony from 1686 to 1702. And after the two territories merged into a united Jersey under a single royal governor, the last of whom under British rule happened to be Ben Franklin's son William, the town served with Burlington as the alternate provincial capital.

The name of the place underwent some permutations during this time. In the deed in which, on December 8, 1651, local Indians ceded the point of land at the mouth of the Raritan to a man named Augustine Herman, the location was called

Ompoge. Thirteen years later, as Pickersgill tells us, the land was transferred to another party and was remarked to be located at "Arthur Cull, or Emboyle." In 1666, the name was written "Amboyle" and this became transformed into "Ambo" and "Ambo Point" and then "Amboy." The "Perth" was added to honor an early Scottish proprietor of East Jersey, James Drummond, the fourth Earl of Perth.

Evidence of old British rule lies all about the town, in, for example, the imposing structure of Proprietary House on Kearny Avenue, about a block and a half before the street slopes down toward the bay. This is the royal governor's mansion that was built in 1762 from bricks shipped from England (and the house where William Franklin took up residence when he assumed his governorship in 1774). St. Peter's Church, a few blocks up the hill and to the east, was built in 1698 as New Jersey's first Episcopal place of worship. In Barracks Street, just north of the main business district of Smith Street, the British troops were housed.

A number of other historical sites are marked with identifying plaques, such as the ferry slip, recently restored, at the foot of Smith Street, where from the colonial period on through 1963 travelers could cross the Arthur Kill by small ferry to Staten Island and travel across the island to the boat to Battery Park in Manhattan. And Kearny Cottage, on Catalpa Street, near the water, built in 1780 by Commodore Laurence Kearny, a local hero. Here, during a period of plague in New York City, the writer usually regarded as America's first native novelist, Charles Brockden Brown, took refuge for a while. Since New Jersey's tercentennial celebration, a plaque in front of City Hall, where High Street and Market Street intersect at a small traffic circle, announces the dates of the town's tenure as colonial capital. The old Surveyor General's Office lies just off to the side of City Hall.

Kings, dukes, lords, royal governors, surveyors general! We kids growing up here never noticed much of this. It wasn't history but nature that attracted us, namely, the water. The Lenni Lenapes were nearly three hundred years gone when as a child, descending from the rocks onto the pebbly sand at "Nickel Beach" where my parents paid the toll and took me and my brother to swim, I chased horseshoe crabs into the gently lapping waters of the bay, when I wasn't digging in the sand to capture gray crabs no larger than a thumbnail to put in paper cups and later set free into the oncoming tide. Or watching avidly as a friend's father buried potatoes in the sand and built a fire over them and let them bake.

In the forties, before the polio scares cleared the sand of all but sunbathers, the beach was a gathering place for the mostly Jewish—and these mostly the working-class Eastern European Jews rather than our middle-class German Jewish brethren— residents of the part of town south of the business district. A few old wooden piers jutted out into the water, and the walk along the low iron railing that lined the beach was made of broad wooden planks (hard on bicycle tires, was what we boys found). Travel west, along the newly named Sadowski Parkway, you'd see a softball field and next to that the local sewage treatment plant. On hot summer days the fecal odor at this end of the boardwalk was quite noticeable, but that didn't stop cocky Polish kids who lived north of the shopping district from diving off the standpipes that let partially treated waste water into the river.

As we grew older, we not only traveled to the water, we traveled over it, renting rowboats and venturing out into the bay, sometimes rowing to where the large oil tankers dropped their huge anchors, waiting their turn to steam up the Kill to unload their valuable liquid cargo at one of the storage tank farms along the shore. Now and then we rowed out too far, as we did one summer Sunday afternoon when we got caught in a strong out-flowing ocean tide and had to be towed back in to town by a passing motorboat. In our early teenage years, we paid our nickels to ride the ferry across the Arthur Kill over to Staten Island, and, later, paying the low fare on the Rapid Transit Train ("the Rat-Trap," we called it) to the north side of Staten Island to take a second ferry across New York Harbor to Battery Park.

In the past decade, water has played an important role in the restoration of the town's past glory, such as it was, and in adding some luster that it had never before possessed. Tourist buses boasting the sign "Bay City Trolley" roll along Sadowski Parkway, their drivers showing off the point of confluence where the river merges with the bay. Between the restored ferry slip and the docks of the old Raritan Yacht Club a newly restored waterfront, with piers and benches and plenty of parking, a few seafood restaurants, and a constant display of masts and small boats, has been constructed. New condos face east toward the Staten Island shore. Clearly, somebody in City Hall and some developers woke up one morning and agreed with Pindar.

But though the waterfront has been spiffed up and the historical sites restored, many of the landmarks of my private past lie in ruins or have disappeared altogether. Down in my old neighborhood a few blocks from the river, Number Seven School, my old elementary school, is still open for business, but its sooty, dimpled turn-of-the-century fortress-style brick facing gives the impression of a structure only recently excavated from centuries of muck and rust. My old brick and ivy imitation Oxbridge style high school on State Street just below Smith is now an elementary school. The Majestic, our town's premiere movie theater, where we kids used to spend most of our Saturday afternoons and where, traditionally, our high school held its commencement ceremonies, has been transformed into "The Cathedral," a gospel church from which of a Sunday morning huge crowds of black families overflow, all of them dressed in what we used to call Sunday "finery," hats, gloves, suits, shoes, scarves, cloaks that call to mind the costume shop of a large movie lot.

And in the past fifty years fire has taken its toll. The old Parker House Hotel on Smith Street, named after a family that settled in East Jersey in the late seventeenth century, was long ago destroyed by flames. The four-story YMHA building that once stood a block north of the main street, with swimming pool in the basement, gymnasium and auditorium on the first floor, and a wired-in rooftop space for outdoor sports also burned, together with the oriental-turreted orthodox synagogue alongside it. The narrow tobacco and candy store owned by my grandparents a few blocks west on Smith Street has disappeared into a row of bazaar-like scarf and hat and food shops. The saloon next door that tinged the air on the block with the overpowering scent of sour yeast closed its doors before I reached the end of my elementary school education (though I don't have to strain memory's ear too much to hear the distinctive sound of beer kegs bouncing out of the back of the brewery truck onto the curb and rolling into the saloon).

The catalog of change and transformation goes on and on. On the site of Golub's fancy produce store now stands a bodega. At Arnesen Square, where of a Sunday morning the archetypal kosher delicatessen drew customers from all around the county, there is a vacant lot. The horse trough at the square has been turned into a large stone flower pot. Parnes' Bakery, another Sunday morning magnet for Perth Amboy's Jews, has become a panicería. The grammar school, on the site of the old British barracks, now houses the offices of the local board of education.

Over on the river the old sewage plant is gone, and a brand-new, Michael Graves style elementary school, named after my late cousin Robert Wilentz, former chief justice of the New Jersey Supreme Court, has risen nearby. On Smith Street, Lerner Shops, where my mother worked for a while in the dress department, has another name. The newsstand across the street, where Barney the blind proprietor was a fixture for us schoolboys, has disappeared, and Barney and his sighted wife who worked alongside him are long dead. Though the apartments and narrow houses I remember calling home, none of them ever more than a two-minute walk from the water, still stand, with other lives lived within them now, other languages spoken.

Oh, Ompoge! Oh, Emboyle! My mother's family settled in Perth Amboy early in the twentieth century, her grandparents having emigrated during some political unrest from Rumania. Her mother was born here. Her father emigrated from Russia before World War One. My father arrived from the other side of the world to court my mother in the late thirties. I was born in Perth Amboy General Hospital, now the Raritan Bay Medical Center, in 1940. My parents now lie next to each other in a cemetery west of town, a long, long walk from the rejuvenating water.

Originally published in Preservation

AN ARTIST'S ADOBE

I've never made a religious pilgrimage, but the trip my wife and I took recently to Georgia O'Keeffe's eighteenth-century adobe house in Abiquiu, New Mexico, was, for us, a journey to a shrine.

We had been preparing for this trip for years, ever since I published a novel based in part on O'Keeffe's life. My wife, Kristin O'Shee, a dancer, choreographed movement to accompany portions of the text. We were not prepared for the natural beauty of the mesas of the Chama River Valley north of Abiquiu. This is where O'Keeffe roamed around in her car, stopping here and there along the way to paint on summer days so hot she often took her breaks by lying in the shade beneath her vehicle. This is where you see that O'Keeffe, lauded as an American innovator and modernist and visionary, is much more of a realist than she is usually taken for.

As we drove along highway 84 northwest from Santa Fe, the spare and luminous landscape that O'Keeffe made so compelling in her work seemed to give off an added resonance and heightened our sense that we had set out on no ordinary tour.

There was nothing ordinary in how O'Keeffe found her way to Abiquiu, a small village about 50 miles from Santa Fe. It was 1929, and after years in New York as a highly regarded artist and the wife of Alfred Stieglitz, the photographer, she gave in to her long-suppressed need for some breathing space and new landscapes. A decade before, when she was in her early thirties, O'Keeffe and her youngest sister had passed through New Mexico while on a train trip to Colorado. She decided that she would spend a summer in that place where she recalled the distinctive quality of the light.

So O'Keeffe, by then in her forties, took a trip west in the company of Rebecca Strand, wife of the photographer Paul Strand. Arriving in Taos, she met the notorious American eccentric and arts patron Mabel Dodge Luhan, who helped her to settle in for a season of painting. Luhan—talkative and overbearing—grew quickly tiresome, but the summer trip to New Mexico became a custom. During one of these sojourns, O'Keeffe found herself traveling along an unpaved highway to an old dude ranch about 20 miles northwest of Abiquiu. The place was called Ghost Ranch, and there she rented a house and painted every summer for more than a decade.

While living on the property, O'Keeffe heard of an abandoned adobe house on the edge of a low north-facing mesa in Abiquiu. The house had been built by a Mexican general named José María Chávez in a village ceded by the Mexican government to a small group of Indians who had converted to Christianity. The three-acre property had irrigation rights—extremely important in this dry, high desert—and an overgrown, untended garden to prove it. When O'Keeffe first inquired about it, she thought the $6,000 asking price too high. The owner, a descendant of Chávez, wouldn't come down in price and willed the old ruin to the Archdiocese of New Mexico.

After his death, the church authorities were at first reluctant to sell the property, even though the buildings and the grounds were in great disrepair. O'Keeffe persisted, and in 1945, the year before Alfred Stieglitz died, they allowed her to buy the house for a token $10. She turned the job of renovation over to her friend and secretary Maria Chabot, mailing many of her ideas for the house from New York where she was settling Stieglitz's estate.

From 1949 onward, O'Keeffe made New Mexico her permanent residence, spending summer and autumn at Ghost Ranch and spring in the Abiquiu house that Chabot had restored to a spare and pristine state.

The moment we stepped through the gate, Kris and I experienced what must have been O'Keeffe's immediate pleasure at first seeing the property. Behind the high walls that protected the adobe structure early in its history from marauding Indians (and now from passionate tourists without the necessary advance reservations for the tour) is a large grassy sward and several rows of green trees and plants and vegetable plots. These stand in stark contrast to the dry, brown, cracked earth and hills that surround this little version of Eden.

The house itself is a low adobe structure, one of those innumerable northern New Mexico residences that seem to have risen from the desert soil and may at any moment disappear back into the earth. Our tour guide, Monica Bittman, a Czech-born painter who had immigrated to the region, showed us the handprints of the local women who had smoothed out the layer of cement on the exterior of the house—a protection against the pounding winter rains. Then she directed our attention inside.

As we saw by looking through the south-facing living room, the floors within are traditional adobe mud, too fragile, Monica assured us, to accommodate visitors. The living room walls, also made of plastered mud, were bare, except for a small version of O'Keeffe's monumental painting *Sky Above Clouds*, which hangs in the Chicago Art Institute. On a shelf in one corner sat a stereo system that O'Keeffe imported from New York, along with a technician to install it properly so that she might enjoy her regular evenings of classical music.

Next, Monica led the dozen or so in our tour group to the patio through a small archway where O'Keeffe's gardener, Esteban Suazo, kept his tools. Some of them are still there, hanging on pegs. In the patio, we saw the black door that O'Keeffe so often used in her paintings, and the huge elk skull mounted at the side of the old house's original entrance, where Indians and Spaniards stooped to enter through a small door within the door. After stepping into the house, we found ourselves in the laundry room, and then in the kitchen to its left—a model '50s kitchen. O'Keeffe's penchant for the practical led her to buy the newest cooking and washing appliances, including a dishwasher. All the appliances, cookware, jars full of dried herbs, a set of sparely elegant Tiffany glasses, and the cleaning fluids and utensils remain just as they were when O'Keeffe left the house, blind and frail, two years before her death at the age of ninety-eight in 1986.

Off to one side of the kitchen is the "Indian room," where local tribesmen came to trade during the years General Chávez lived there. And from the kitchen we could see the long living room and its mud floors from another angle.

"My grandmother cooked here," said Cindy Gallegos, a young woman who had been assisting Monica with the tour. "I used to play in this kitchen all the time when I was a child."

"And now, the studio," Monica said, preparing to lead us into the sanctum sanctorum. We left the kitchen through another door and stepped onto a large outdoor patio, where some of the many piles of rocks and stones that O'Keeffe collected from the river decorated the otherwise bare space.

O'Keeffe's studio, on the other side of the patio, was somewhat disappointing. Unlike Faulkner's study at Rowanoak in Oxford, Mississippi, or Melville's upstairs writing room at Arrowhead in Pittsfield, Massachusetts, the room doesn't give the impression that the artist has just finished work and stepped out for a moment. Though O'Keeffe's spare bed beneath the windowsill is still there, the original mud floor has been covered with carpeting, and the only art in sight was a very rough canvas, a view of the Washington Monument that O'Keeffe painted with the help of an assistant after a visit late in life to the nation's capital.

How might it have looked? "The studio looks like an attic—it always does when I work," O'Keeffe wrote to a friend in the early 1950s. "One ten-foot table is full of canvas and stretchers and hammers and tacks. The palette is on a table I can wheel about—another one is on the windowsill." It's a disappointment that the foundation has apparently decided to give the impression of the retired O'Keeffe rather than the working artist.

But the last stop on the tour called her back to us. It was O'Keeffe's sleeping quarters, the bedroom she occupied toward the end of her life. Though visitors are only allowed to stare at it through a window on the north side of the house, the scene is intensely personal: a white bed, a glimpse of the bathroom plumbing behind a half opened door. On the walls there is nothing but a small piece of sculpture, the hand of a Buddha that O'Keeffe bought as a souvenir while on a trip to Asia. Upon awakening she could see it beckoning to her, and then, we imagined, she would look beyond it to the marvelous hills and canyons that make up the world outside.

"I wish you could see what I see outside the window," she wrote to the painter Arthur Dove back in New York. "The earth pink and yellow cliffs to the north—the full pale moon about to go down in an early morning lavender sky behind a very long beautiful tree-covered mesa to the west—pink and purple hills in front and the scrubby fine dull green cedars—and a feeling of much space…I wish you could see it."

Originally published in the New York Times.

GOLD COUNTRY DRIFTING

A Tuesday morning in mid-August, and my wife and I are standing on a water-slicked hard rock floor some six hundred feet beneath the surface of a hill of brown-gold sun-worn grass in Sutter Creek, California, in the heart of the heart of Gold Rush country. A fourth generation miner named Charlie Chatfield, a trim grey-bearded, flat-nosed man in miner's apron, hard hat and short sleeves, directs our attention, as he swings the beam of his battery-powered lantern in the same direction, to the barely visible mineral formation on the wall of the mine shaft.

We're wearing deep red hard hats ourselves, and dressed for the cool air of the mine—about sixty degrees year-round, Charlie has informed us. In California summers, growing more and more swelled by the heat, this might in fact be the coolest place in the state! Though the cool air in the depths of the mine is a welcome but unintended consequence of our trip, whose purpose is to find a few days diversion *in*land, for a change, rather than in the coastal strip where we usually spend most of our summer time, and in a region far from the roaming crowds of plush Napa and Sonoma.

So here we are *under*land, underground, and Charlie's pointing out something rather dramatic about how to find gold.

"The quartz contains the gold," Charlie tells us, keeping his beam on the vein of quartz we can now see running through the so-called green stone (the hard rock) of the shaft. "We follow the drift, or the direction, of the vein of the gold-bearing ore, and that's where we drill…And you can see it drifting…" (he swings his beam of light against the wall of the shaft and moves down into the shaft and we follow) "…all the way down here, and across the ceiling and down below…"

Following the drift of the gold-bearing quartz!

That's how we started our week, taking the easy eastward drive out of Sacramento, where we'd stayed with family for a few days, up into the foothills of the Sierras. (As a journalist friend of mine, a long-time northern Californian guy put it, when I told him of our impending trip, "Good idea. Napa and Sonoma are maxed out! The Gold Country's twenty-five years behind them, and that's great!")

Our first stop, only an hour out of Sacramento, was an old sawmill on the banks of the South Fork of the American River, in the tiny settlement of Coloma. As most California school kids know—sixty thousand of them troop through here each year on educational tours—Coloma was the location of the first gold strike in the state. Ah, that day in 1848, when New Jersey native James Marshall, who had drifted across the country from the east and opened the mill, caught the glint of the gold-flecked quartz in the mineral tailings of his mill race! Within a year hundreds of thousands of would-be golden millionaires swarmed across these hills, panning in the streams and rivers, and digging holes in the hillsides, following the drift of the gold-bearing rocks that spread south from Coloma along the ridges of the foothills almost all the way to Yosemite. Searching for a heart of gold!

John Sutter, Marshall's former mill partner, headed south along the line of these hills to build another sawmill. And pan and dig. Sutter traveled on horseback, with wagons loaded with equipment. It took him awhile. Today it's an easy drive from Coloma, a little more than an hour due south on State Highway 49, to Sutter Creek, where we would meet Charlie Chatfield and take our tour of the Sutter Gold Mine. And then emerge from underground to spend the rest of the day lazing about on the balcony of the old Imperial Hotel in nearby Amador City, taking the measure of a warm day above ground in a town that minus the paved two-lane Highway 49 running through it, and minus the power lines, might well be something like the hamlet where some miners hit it big, and others dug themselves into exhaustion and oblivion.

Some facts about the gold business stayed with me as we sat in the stillness of the afternoon, and some of these I probably won't ever let go. The drastic ratio between the number of tons of ore you have to mine and the tiny amount of gold this yields (only about half an ounce to ten ounces at most from a ton of rock). Having inspected the drills, some by now museum pieces, others still operating in the still operating mine, I found myself thinking about the bone-jouncing ratcheting of the steel machines and the multi-millions of shattering instants in the arms and legs of the miners. No seekers of wealth or truth, whether bankers or sailors or poets or philosophers, have put so much injurious labor into the production of so little! And yet Marshall's discovery made for so much. For without the gold rush, that fever to become an instant millionaire that haunts most Americans from school-age on upward, a fever handed down from the first European explorers who sought out a fresh continent, a place free of sin and filled with impossible possibilities, a land with fabled sidewalks and cities of gold, how many immigrants would have rushed west to make California the state that it became?

James Marshall didn't know it, and couldn't have known it, but when he spied those first flecks of gold in the mill race he was spying on the future of the state, of the country, of you and me.

That night we had an excellent meal in a new restaurant called Taste in the winery town of Plymouth, only a few miles back up the road toward Coloma, and drove south the next morning to the little hill-town of Murphys that still has a certain post-Gold Rush glamour upon it. You can take the measure of both sides of its main street in about twenty minutes, or stroll up the road through the little town park and cross the bridge over the creek and walk another mile or so up the road to the Ironstone Winery and feel the weight of city life falling away as you stride. Or, if you've struck it somewhat rich in your good city life you can repair, as we did, to a luxurious bed-and-breakfast on a hilltop about four miles east of town, and sit on your private patio and sink down deep into a shaft that leads all the way to the bottom of restfulness and enjoy a sort of waking meditation.

A hilltop in Murphys! What a fine place to pan for stillness, to mine for rest. Given the peace that arises from the countryside, two days and nights in Murphys were worth their weight in gold. Bird song, bird song, bird song. At night a vast drift of stars.

And stillness in early morning, with the air flocked with more bird song. Hummingbirds, too, hovering, then zumming away like large bees. Pine needles shimmering in the wind that flows like water. As the sun rises three hilltops become visible to the north, the tailings of gold mines trimming them like the heads of hip young school kids with layered haircuts. A quartet of deer, three does and a buck precariously bedecked with two tender points, skitter past. The official bed-and-breakfast mouse-catcher pads by on silent feet.

We then padded down to the patio below the balcony for a lavish breakfast prepared in the restaurant-grade kitchen by the owner and his wife—with fig-and-lemon scones nearly as light as air and blue corn pancakes to match the near-turquoise morning sky.

Feeling not so much drifting as pulled—that's how we find ourselves two days later driving south again on Highway 49, an hour and a half or so south of Murphys, taking the eastern turnoff onto mountain Highway 120 and making our way up and around the curves to the village of Groveland and then rolling into the Stanislaus National Forest to the northern entrance to Yosemite. Only a few hours from Sacramento, less than half a day from San Francisco, and we've arrived in another kingdom, the California of towering rock and sky-high tree that rivals even the myths of the enriching possibilities of the Gold Rush.

Visitors, vastly outnumbering the population of those prospectors of another era, stream in from countries around the world and swarm through the forest, camping and tramping, biking and rafting, rubber-necking in a geological Eden. Mid-afternoon in Yosemite, and you can imagine the great national park as honey and the tourists as ants, all of us feeling reduced to that size when we look up at the cliff-sides that bound the valley. That sense of wonder you felt when you first recognized yourself as a solitary creature in a world full of natural amazements—here is the place—a couple of million years behind Napa and Sonoma—where you can restore it, recharge it, or, wonder upon wonder, if you are such a person who has lived bereft of the connection to mountains, forests, stream, and sky, find it for the first time.

We have dinner that night in the elegant dining room of the historic Ahwanee Hotel, with its thirty-four-foot high ceilings and floor-to-ceiling windows overlooking the park giving the feel of dining with Citizen Kane rather than John Muir. The extensive menu included a delicious mustard-crusted sea bass, grilled Kobe beef, pan-roasted line-caught halibut, and a savory organic tofu and vegetable curry—and for dessert, banana wrapped in phyllo with chocolate bits. Ah, wilderness!

The next day, we wake up early enough to find something resembling solitude, and from our balcony of a grand old hotel in the middle of the valley, watch the first light fill the visible patches of sky above the towering cliffs. As morning slowly settles like brilliant mist toward the valley floor, we make our way to the trailhead and begin our climb up the 30 percent grade of the trail to Vernal Falls. A few troops of college students carrying their school flags race past us to the fork that leads high up to Half Dome. But on our gentle climb to the falls it's mostly couples and solitary hikers we meet, all of us agreed, like pilgrims on the way to the Pearly Gates, that we've got a good purpose and don't need to talk about it. The few words we do hear come in Japanese and Chinese, Basque and French, and German.

After an hour or so we stop where the trail bows out over cascading water just below the falls to sip from our own liquid stash. It's not that we're tired from this climb, but more that we'd like to string it out as long as we can. To pause here, just short of the long set of steps leading up through the mist of the thundering falls, surrounded by the rocks and rills celebrated in our national music, gives us the illusion that we might just have caught the real drift of our own lives. Never have we traveled so short a distance to gain so much. Oh, Yosemite, unlike those early prospectors who arrived along the ridges of the hills to the northwest and hunkered down at the gushing streams desperate to make their fortunes, we're not panning for gold. Here we discover that if time is gold, if light is gold, and air is gold, we're richer than ever we imagined.

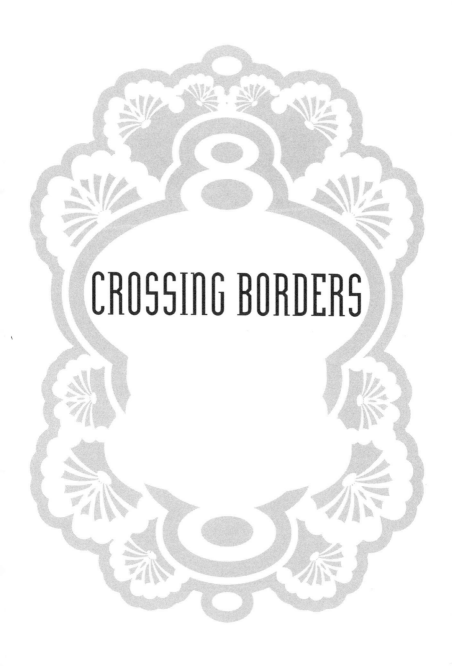

CROSSING BORDERS

PORT OF ENTRY

In *Secondary Inspection:* Sonja—her real name—is breathing hard, straining, pulling, ready as she'll ever be to get to the business at hand. George, her partner (not his real name), struggles a bit to keep her from running wildly across the parking lot.

Please! please! Let me at it! Let me at it!

You can almost hear her voice in her surging, lunging movements, the whining, begging, straining noises on her red lips.

I want it! I want to play! I want to play so bad!

Okay, okay, okay, girl, George says, racing with her toward the automobile, a huge red Chevy Silverado that's just pulled in to the lot.

Two men in blue wait at the driver's side as a short, lean dark-haired fellow in a windbreaker climbs down from behind the wheel. They immediately place him in handcuffs, take him by the arm, and lead him into the nearby doorway. A female inspector in blue helps from the car a Mexican woman holding as she might a bundle of kindling a stiff-limbed child, obviously mentally handicapped, about four years old, and behind them scramble two more children, tugging little suitcases after them. The handicapped girl shrieks, afraid, confused.

Go get it, girl, George urges Sonja on, and the obedient dog, a trim, brindled hunter with a Belgian pedigree, sniffs and snorts her way around the vehicle, nearly tearing the leash out of her master's hand as she surges toward the right side of the rear bumper.

Oh, whoa! her master shouts. Get it girl get it girl get it get it get it!

That's it, he says to the others in blue gathering around him, half a dozen Customs and Border Protection inspectors, all of them just as enthusiastic as the drug-sniffing dog.

It's Saturday night at the San Ysidro Port of Entry, one of the busiest border crossings in the world. (In a typical month, the inspectors here will see over a million vehicles and more than half a million pedestrians, with the total number of people inspected coming to over three million.)

Eight o'clock, in the Secondary Inspection area, behind the main administration building. A mélange of men and women in blue uniforms, some Customs, some Immigration and Naturalization inspectors, the majority of them former navy, army, air force, marines, sheriff's deputies, and patrolmen. At the south end of the lot, the ground floor of the Port of Entry's main offices, with holding cells, administrative offices, a lunchroom, and, in the front, the glassed-in command post known as "the fish bowl," where computers and television cameras and radios allow the inspectors working there to watch just about every vehicle and individual moving from Mexico toward the American side of the border line. Near the back of the Secondary Inspection area, a small glassed-in office where resident aliens who need to travel beyond the twenty-five mile limit allowed in their regular permits must go to get new papers. A small line of petitioners standing at the booth. At the rear of the lot, an area where dozens of seized motor vehicles are parked, waiting to be towed to a government impoundment lot.

This pilgrim arrives just as Sonja begins her search for drugs. The pilgrim watches, while talking with G.S., a senior inspector. Medium height, greying mustache and greying fringe of hair, pistol at his hip, G.S. speaks in a warm, reassuring manner about the operation unfolding in front of us.

The dogs are usually right, he says. The car is loaded.

With?

Probably marijuana. But let's see.

G.S. and the pilgrim stroll over to the vehicle where, over the shoulders of the curious inspectors, they watch one man in blue work with a tire iron to separate the bumper from the body of the vehicle.

Whoa! the dog handler shouts. Good girl, good girl! He praises excitable Sonja as she dances around the bumper.

With a wrenching screech of steel, the bumper comes loose, and man and dog dig about in the space it has left.

Yes! the handler cries. Yes! yes! Good girl! good girl!

The dog burrows its nose into a stash of neatly pressed bricks of marijuana wrapped in plastic and taped tightly closed.

They put the stuff in trash compactors, G.S. explains to the pilgrim.

A Customs agent in plain clothes arrives to take a picture of the car.

Can you believe that the guy put his family in the car like that? G.S. is disgusted.

I can't believe people do that to each other. With a handicapped child in the car, no less.

The pilgrim mulls this over, the possibility that drug smugglers have no shame.

Maybe they put pressure on him, the pilgrim says.

Driving a vehicle like that, he's probably already up to his ears in corruption. G.S. looks around at the sound of the child. But it's only Sonja, returning to her temporary quarters in a Customs vehicle on a distant section of the lot.

Lead or gold, another inspector says. That's the choice they give them sometimes. A bullet in the head, or they go to work for them.

It's lousy, the inspector says. (When someone detects a load of drugs, the inspectors gather around like kids at a fire.)

It can be funny, too, another man says. One time I spotted this guy, a well-known drug smuggler, but someone we never could catch, driving through Primary and I said, Gotcha!

He leaned out of his car and laughed.

No, hombre, he said, it's my day off. I'm clean!

So I said to him, Well, you have to make it through every time, and I just have to catch you once. So I had the laugh on him.

A lot of funny things happen. We had this married couple in Secondary, and I asked the guy to open the glove compartment. He wouldn't do it. So I had him and his wife step out of the vehicle and I opened the glove compartment myself. The law mandates this kind of inspection without a warrant. We can do these things that no other law enforcement people can do without a warrant. So I open it. And there's a pair of women's underpants. The wife saw them, too, and from the way she looked you knew right away that they weren't her underpants. Sorry about that. And I heard a story, but didn't see it myself, about an inspector who opened the glove compartment and saw a face staring out at him—the kid was in a secret compartment built at the back of the engine.

A female inspector—S.G., in her early thirties, Mexican American, severely carved face that shows her Indian blood— pushes a supermarket cart up to the car and the inspectors unload a dozen or so of the bricks into the cart. The inspector then pushes the cart up across the narrow traffic lanes that separate the main Customs lot from one across the way, and into the small building with an evidence room and holding cells.

They count the bricks and under G.S.'s supervision the woman takes a knife and cuts into one of them. She's putting real muscle into it—the stuff is packed tight and hard.

Looks like someone cutting into Gouda cheese, the pilgrim says.

It's marijuana Gouda, G.S. says.

The pilgrim allows himself the favor of a sniff test.

Not very strong odor, but enough to convince his old pot-head's nostril hairs.

A lot of sage, G.S. says without moving his nose any closer to the brick than it was before.

Of course, the pilgrim says. Diluted quite a bit.

The woman weighs each brick, and then cuts in for a sample for laboratory testing. Another young inspector, a man about twenty-five or so, then packs the bricks into a cardboard evidence box and marks the box and seals it. The box goes in to the evidence room for storage.

The policy here is zero tolerance, G.S. explains. If we find a small amount on you and it's clearly for personal use, we cite you for a misdemeanor. Five thousand dollar fine, but it usually gets knocked down to five hundred for a first offense. But if you're clearly smuggling, like this load, then you're in more trouble. Of course, when you go before the judge around here, the kind of sentence you get isn't really terribly discouraging.

The pilgrim ponders the policy of zero tolerance, thinks of the friends he has who smoke marijuana in a regular way, wonders what they would say if they witnessed this scene. Well, he knows. Make it legal, they would say.

The pilgrim asks the young inspector his name.

Don't use my name, he says. I want to live.

Are you worried about—?

The smugglers have spies everywhere, the young inspector tells the pilgrim. Don't use my name.

I won't use anyone's name in the story, the pilgrim says. That will make things equal.

What is your story? the inspector says.

A story about the port of entry, the pilgrim says. A day in the life of. Or a night.

It's interesting here all the time, the inspector says. Day or night. Of course, Saturday nights are the wildest, usually. But anything can happen here any time of day, any day of the week. The pilgrim nods, takes this in. The inspector goes on: I love this work. I can't wait to wake up and put on my uniform and come to work.

You have time to go home and sleep? the woman says.

I'm on overtime, the inspector says to the pilgrim. Like almost everybody. Two eight-hour shifts back to back. So you go home for a couple of hours and then you try to sleep and then you get up and get dressed and come back here.

Do you dream about the job?

I do, the man says.

I do, the woman says. There's always one car that I didn't get to. I worry about that one car, the one with all the drugs, and I let it go through.

I dream about opening suitcases, another inspector says to the pilgrim as he walks out onto the Customs lot again.

Not me, G.S. says. I sleep soundly.

One suitcase after another, the other man says.

G.S. laughs. We walk up to the watch booth at the end of the lot. Gathered here are a half dozen inspectors, men, women, young, old, some with grey hair, paunches, others slender young men a year or two out of the army or the marines, several women, white and black and Latina, one a K-9 officer telling dog stories, another young woman, a recent hire from Florida with a blond ponytail, pretty narrow face talking about a load of marijuana she caught earlier in the evening. Every now and then someone checks the rotation list for the next hour.

There are three main rotations for each inspector, time on the lot helping with inspections of vehicles, time at the pedestrian border crossing in the next building over, and time at the inspection booth on the line.

I'm on my second shift today, a tall, Chicano fellow in blue says to the pilgrim.

It's 8:15 and I feel like I'm never going home again.

What's to go home for? another inspector says. My wife left for Texas and I'm staying in an empty house.

That's the job, the tall fellow says to the pilgrim. It doesn't do good things to marriages.

Are you married? the pilgrim asks.

The inspector shakes his head.

The pilgrim edges over toward one of the women and asks, as delicately as he knows how, about whether or not she dates men on the job.

She shakes her head. My uncle works in Customs back home, she says. He warned me about stuff like that.

Another young woman—brown-skinned, hair pulled back—standing nearby concurs.

But I don't even have time, even if I wanted to. I work double shifts, I go home and sleep and come back to the job. On my days off I go to the gym and shop for food and that's about it.

8:20 p.m. From somewhere in the back of the parking lot a young Mexican woman is led in handcuffs toward the main building.

An inspector wanders over.

Jerry Garcia? he says, staring at the pilgrim's curly hair and salt-and-pepper beard.

There's talk about look-alikes. The pilgrim says he had a tour of the INS offices earlier in the week from a supervisor who was a dead-ringer for Dan Ackroyd. The inspector says there's a guy works here, don't know what shift he's on this week, looks just like the actor…Robert…? what's his name?

Robert?

Duvall! the inspector emphatically remembers the name.

The pilgrim nods. You live long enough, you see enough people, things begin to resemble one another, even as their differences become more pronounced. He ponders this philosophical consideration for a moment longer in the relative calm that has settled over the inspection area. In the distance, there is always the steady roar of tires, the winding up and winding down of engines, an occasional horn. But this seems to be the normal level of tranquillity here. He ponders this too, and then hears shouts coming from the direction of the inspection booths out in front of the main building.

Six inspectors in blue come running in alongside a Honda with a brown-faced man behind the wheel. They direct him into a parking space and then remove him from the car, taking his keys and tossing them onto the roof of the vehicle. Someone calls for a K-9, but before the dog and trainer arrive the inspectors pop the trunk and, as if in a magic act, a stocky fellow in a plaid shirt leaps up out of his hiding place and blinks against the light.

An agent in plain clothes, his gold Customs badge dangling on a loop over his stomach, comes over with a camera and asks the man to pose. The man smiles an embarrassed smile. Click—he's on file. His smile quickly fades as the agent leads him in to the building to be placed in a holding cell.

8:30 p.m. A lull in the action. The pilgrim can hardly believe that he has been out here only half an hour. Lives have flashed by. People, free when they drove up to the Primary Inspection booths, now see prison in the near future. Children will lose their fathers; wives, their husbands.

Some inspectors are talking about food, whether to go to McDonald's or Burger King.

An inspector rolls past, pushing a shopping cart full of boxes of smuggled shoes.

8:35 p.m. A car pulls into Secondary, the driver immediately asked to step out and place his hands on the vehicle. A stolen vehicle. Driver led away in handcuffs. He's no sooner gone than another vehicle pulls up with a British fellow at the wheel and an American in the passenger seat.

Inspectors swarm over the car.

Can the driver please open the trunk?

The trunk pops open. And out pop a man and a boy, blinking against the light, illegal aliens who are immediately led away.

A lean gray-haired inspector watches this and says to the pilgrim, They'll claim they didn't know it was a crime. But it is, whether they knew it or not. They thought they were being cool, smuggling people across.

8:40 p.m. Female inspector, from K-9, talks to pilgrim about her eighteen years of service, loves her job, no complaints, except that she can't take her dog home with her. (INS dog handlers can take their animals home.)

Would-be people smugglers led away.

8:50 p.m. Inspectors walk in a short brown-skinned man in handcuffs from the Primary Inspection area. The man tried to pass through inspection booth by walking on the far side of a recreational vehicle. Inspector spotted him at once. He has no papers.

8:54 p.m. A family walks quietly along behind a burly gray-haired INS inspector from the INS booth in the rear of the Secondary Inspection area.

The inspector raises his voice, saying, You didn't bring your documents along? I asked you to get them out of the car! You are a rocket scientist, aren't you? At least you can make up a good story *before* you get caught!

The man holds up his hands in resignation as the inspector leads him and his family into the building for further investigation.

9:00 p.m. East County Fire Department ambulance arrives in Secondary, awaiting the arrival of a Tijuana ambulance so the crew can transfer an injured U.S. citizen to a local hospital.

9:02 p.m. Car pulls into Secondary, inspectors ask the driver to step out, one inspector removes several sacks of potatoes from rear of vehicle while another calls for K-9.

Dog arrives, aggressively sniffs around the wheelbases, fenders, lights, grill, and then leaps inside the car, sniffs, sniffs.

Nothing here.

9:05 p.m. Driver and car released.

9:07 p.m. Tijuana ambulance arrives with woman on stretcher, ribs bruised in auto accident over the border. Child with her has bruised face. Drivers transfer patient to East County ambulance.

9:10 p.m. A lull. G.S. and pilgrim talk about the prevalence of drugs in the United States, the breakdown of the family, discipline, ethics, morality at home—and in the courts.

Typical law enforcement lament. He arrests them and watches the courts set them free.

9:20 p.m. Ambulances depart.

9:29 p.m. Another lull. G.S. continues conversation with pilgrim about decline in American life, particularly in education. Tells of an applicant who on his application spelled "family" two different ways, both incorrect.

Customs averages about one drug seizure an hour. Here comes a car. The dog picked it out of the line of traffic stacked up at the Primary Inspection booths. Driver out. Inspectors pour over it, with Sonja in the lead. Someone pops the hood. Bricks of marijuana carelessly stuffed along the engine block. K-9 officer lets out whoops of joy, encouraging the dog.

Good girl, good girl, good girl, whacks her with a rolled up towel, yields the towel to the dog, and leads her away to the back of the inspection area.

Good girl, good girl! His voice fades away into the noise of the traffic.

(**Interlude with Document**:

Position Description: Immigration Inspector

I.   *Introduction:*

> As an immigration inspector, the incumbent performs one or more of the following duties in support of certain federal laws. In addition, arrests and detains criminal aliens for other law enforcement agencies pursuant to warrants of arrest.

II. *Major Duties and Responsibilities:*

1. Conducts inspection of all classes of applicants for admission to the United States. Performs initial inspection with the aim of quickly determining, by questioning and observing the individual and by reviewing his or her identifying papers, whether an applicant may be admitted without further formality or whether there are questions or indications of problems that require more detailed examination and require referral to other inspectors who perform a more detailed inspection. As necessary, based on referral from a Primary Inspector, makes a secondary (more detailed) inspection of applicants who require more intensive questioning concerning citizenship, admissibility, purpose of travel, entry documents, and other information. Carries the inspection process in questionable cases to conclusion. Requests and collects maintenance of status and departure bonds. Refers applicants for exclusion hearings. Initiates procedures to fine commercial carriers for transporting documentarily deficient aliens into the United States.

   Initiates administrative and criminal proceedings under appropriate sections of U.S. law, including section 274 of the Immigration and Nationality Act.

2. Adjudicates a wide variety of applications for various immigration privileges and benefits that are processed at the ports-of-entry. Works on applications involving novel and complex application of law and regulation; completes the more complex cases assigned before review by supervisory officers, senior inspectors or immigration inspectors (special operations). Interviews individuals as necessary for confirming information found in applications.

3. Interprets and/or furnishes guidance and advice regarding I&N laws, regulations, and other service policy to inspector trainees, seasonal

*and/or part-time inspectors, and officers of other federal inspectional
agencies who perform immigration inspection functions.*

4. *Gathers, makes use of, and disseminates intelligence information
to other law enforcement officers or refers the information to the
immigration inspector (intelligence) or the immigration inspector
(special operations) if either officer is stationed at the port.*

*Serves as the Service representative in a liaison capacity with
local officials in seeking their cooperation, when necessary or
desirable, to further the proper administration of the immigration
laws. Detains and refers to the appropriate agency any person who
is the subject of a local, state or federal arrest warrant or who, from
the information gathered, may be subject to arrest by local, state, or
federal authorities.*

5. *Conducts, for the U.S. Customs Service, the inspection and
examination of arriving persons, baggage, merchandise, and
other items and, where there is vehicular traffic, the conveyances
in which any or all of these are being transported to the United
States. This includes determining the dutiability of merchandise and
verifying the merchandise in a carrier's possession against invoices,
bills of lading, or other documents. Conducts inspection for the
Public Health Service and the Plant Quarantine Division of the
Department of Agriculture. Admits eligible persons, merchandise, etc.
not requiring additional processing, but refers cases which present
unusual problems or require additional processing to an officer of the
appropriate agency for disposition.*

6. *Performs other work as needed or assigned such as custodial duties
concerning detained aliens, furnishes guidance, advice, and forms
to the public, assists individuals in completing forms, administers
oaths, collects fees, etc.*

7. *Responsible for the proper use of firearms and physical arrest techniques. Continues to meet the qualification standards for the use of firearms...)*

9:30 p.m. The pilgrim goes out on the line, to a Primary Inspection booth with R.M., a Filipino American, a compactly built man with a manner that goes from friendliness to absolute business in a matter of seconds. The pilgrim was once a man in a booth, when he worked for the New Jersey Turnpike Authority, collecting tolls or handing out trip tickets. He asked no questions of drivers then. You come and go in New Jersey, as in the rest of our country, at your own will. You cross freely from state to state, of course, as well. It's different for R.M.; this job requires that he practice interrogation; interrogation, and a quick, incisive interrogation at that, is the keen edge of the performance of his duty.

The cars are backed up all the way to the "dip" in the roadway on the Tijuana side of the border line. A dozen lanes at least, open. A mix of Customs inspectors and INS inspectors in the booths. (Rotation changes constantly, so that drug smugglers on the other side of the line can't predict which inspector will be posted at what lane, and at what particular time.) The night air is a bit chilly, but inside the booth a fan heats the small space and beneath the roadway a fan sucks in the exhaust fumes from the passing cars.

They monitor us in their own way, R.M. says as he waves the first car up to his booth. And we monitor the incoming cars and people. And our supervisors over in the "fishbowl"—he means that office, all windows facing on the rows of Primary Inspection lanes, on the ground floor of the main building behind us—monitor us. The idea is to move traffic along as quickly as possible, without compromising inspections too much. We have about thirty seconds a car. It's a quick thirty seconds. For honest border crossers, and most of them are, waiting in line can become an ordeal, and thirty seconds multiplied by thousands can make for a long wait at rush hour. For smugglers of drugs or illegal immigrants, thirty seconds can become an eternity.

The pilgrim watches over his shoulder as he punches in to the computer inside the booth the license number of the next vehicle in line. The computer is hooked into a vast network of information from here just a few miles from the Pacific to the heart of the data banks of Washington, D.C. It tells the inspector when the last time the car crossed the border, if it has crossed before, and kicks out information about known felons, aliases, missing persons, runaways, parole violators, etc. So where once the inspector in the booth was a lonely sentinel standing guard against unlawful crossing of his country's border, now the inspector stands as the foremost figure on an electronic border monitored at a number of deep levels behind him.

The first car on R.M.'s watch rolls forward. The occupants appear to be Anglos.

Nationality, sir?

U.S., the driver says.

R.M. waves them on through. By this time the license of the next vehicle has come up on the screen, with no listing of previous border crossings, no flags concerning other violations.

The driver shows a resident alien card and R.M. takes a close look at it.

Where you going? he asks in Spanish. Some inspectors, like R.M., grew up in Spanish-speaking households, but all the inspectors are trained in the language before they go to work here.

Chula Vista, the driver responds.

R.M. waves him through.

(Most of the resident alien traffic that comes through the port of entry is local, people who reside on the Tijuana side and drive in each day to work on the U.S. side in San Diego County and then return home, or U.S. residents who work in Tijuana and come back through at the end of the workday.)

Where to?

San Diego.

R.M. shines his flashlight into the interior of the van, checking the cards the driver has presented in relation to the people inside. Something piques his curiosity. He asks the driver to open the trunk and then walks around the car, bonging his flashlight against the tires and the fenders, listening for the music of a hollowed out space or specially built secret compartment.

Thank you, sir, he says coming back to the driver's side. He waves the car along.

Next car, full of young girls dressed for a party.

Nationality?

U.S., sir, says the driver, smiling hard. Some of the other girls bat their eyelashes at the inspector. Some giggling from the back seat.

No price on what they're smuggling, the pilgrim says to the inspector in a joking way.

R.M. doesn't crack a smile.

You see everything coming through here, he says, waving the car along. If it's human, it comes this way. And animals, too. Snakes, parrots, you name it, we've seen it.

Next car. Full of young German tourists. They're lost, the driver says. They want to get to El Centro.

R.M. gives them directions.

Next car he stops and almost immediately asks the driver to open the trunk.

It's a make they've noticed as popular with drug smugglers,

he explains. A car gets popular, because the mechanics perfect a particular technique of building compartments and so they use the same car for a while. He pokes around in the trunk, moves bags of food around, taps on the bottom, taps his light against the fenders. Then he moves the car along.

The lines out there haven't seemed to have gotten any shorter, despite R.M.'s skill at moving the cars along.

Five cars in a row driven by resident aliens.

Next car he directs to Secondary, because the passenger needs a special permit to travel beyond the San Diego area.

Next car looks odd to him. He closes his lane and walks this car in to Secondary.

Next car—USA.

Next car—resident alien.

Next car—resident alien. R.M. checks all around and taps his light underneath the vehicle.

Where you going?

Chula Vista.

Where you going?

San Diego.

Where you going?

Chula Vista.

Where you headed?

San Diego.

The rhythm of questions and answers must go through his mind at odd hours of the waking day and sleeping night.

San Diego.

Chula Vista.

Sir?

U.S.

Ma'am?

U.S.

Dónde va?

Chula Vista.

Dónde va?

Chula Vista.

Dónde va?

San Diego.

R.M.'s half-hour shift in the booth comes to an end.

Seventeen lanes open now! The port of entry is Saturday night wide! Here in the center of the plaza stands R.T., a tall black navy veteran, working the cars as quickly as they come with a manner as smooth as a jazz baritone singing quirky lyrics at a small club in some great American city. Next, he says to a carload of young girls crossing over from Tijuana. They flirt a little, he chuckles, checks out the tires, the trunk. Another carload of girls coming back from a party, and he laughs with them at some small joke as he flashes his light inside the back seat of their car.

Next to R.T.'s lane the booth is manned by J.P., angular, earnest, tapping his flashlight against the wheel base of a large white van with California license plates. He's a relatively recent recruit, and as self-conscious about the job as he is serious about it.

It's such interesting work, he says. In fact, he tells the pilgrim, I was thinking about calling the *Reader* to see if they would send somebody over to write about this.

The pilgrim watches him perform his good labor, inquiring, applying little psychological tests as the questions and answers go back and forth in the half minute they spend together, inspector and driver. I have some techniques that pay off, J.P. says. Some things I watch for in the eyes, in a face. I guess everybody develops these after a while.

The pilgrim nods, thinking of what great lay psychologists

these inspectors do become, knowing after a while most of the tell-tale signs of good and many of the marks of evil. He's reminded of what Ernest Hemingway once said was the basic equipment of a good writer: a built-in, automatic, shock-proof shit-detector. He watches J.P. work a little while longer, admiring his grace and his intensity, thinking now, in the mood of Hemingway, how this slender dark-haired fellow could, in another life, have passed bulls before his cape instead of cars through his turnstile, and made a good, if a bit shorter, life as a fine matador. Or he might have been a priest, sifting through statements about sin and good gestures. Or perhaps when he leaves this post he'll take up a position as a counselor somewhere, so well-versed he'll be in the difference between lies and truth.

The pilgrim eventually shifts to a booth where a young female Customs inspector has just taken over. Medium-length hair, freckles, the potential for a wonderful smile when she's not working this line. Her weapon juts out at her hip, announcing to the pilgrim that these lanes are not part of the New Jersey Turnpike. The pilgrim tucks up his jacket collar against the chill. He's working on a bit of a headache from the stray exhaust fumes, and his nose is stuffed, his eyes a little runny.

He mentions this to the inspector.

Welcome to the club, she says. You get a cold and it stays around for weeks on this job. The headache will go away pretty quick.

Where are you from? he inquires.

She answers, waving up her first car. All the way from the heart of the country to stand here at this border line.

Nationality, señor? she asks of the first driver.

USA, the driver says.

And the next half hour begins. An INS inspector, short-cropped hair, glasses, rather professorial in looks. Turns out he's a graduate of a major California music school and he's at work on his third symphony. Still working, on his time off from conducting the traffic in these lanes.

Señor? Your nationality, please?

U.S.

And where are you going?

Los Angeles.

The composer checks their papers.

Thank you, señor.

He waves in the next car.

He checks the next.

He waves along the next.

He checks the next three for hidden contraband, drugs, people.

He waves along the next one.

Next one he leads into Secondary, having seen the tell-tale signs of nervousness on the face of a possible smuggler.

(*Interlude with Document, Continued*:

III. Factor Level Descriptions:

1. *Knowledge required by position:*

    -*Thorough and full technical knowledge and understanding of current immigration and nationality laws, regulations, precedent decisions, policies, and procedures applicable to the inspection and examination functions, including procedures for referring applicant for exclusion hearings, as necessary.*

    -*Knowledge and skill in interview techniques. Must use diplomacy, be tactful, resourceful, and discreet in dealing with and eliciting information from applicants and possess the ability to comprehend and correlate gathering facts.*

    -*Thorough knowledge of rules of evidence and administrative procedures in taking sworn statements. Knowledge of areas of law concerning search and seizure, civil rights, arrest authority, and constitution.*

-Must possess keen insight into human behavior and make accurate discerning decisions based on examination of documents presented, responses to questions, appearance of applicants, their mannerisms, as well as their other actions and reactions.

-Broad knowledge of all Service functions in order to recognize, develop, and refer for appropriate action, information of value to other operational areas.

-Basic knowledge of current Customs and other federal inspection agency laws as they relate to assigned duties...)

10:30 p.m. The pilgrim hooks up with the K-9 team coming up toward the booths, to make inspections out in the lanes. This is what on this job they call "pre-primary." The lead K-9 officer races along with his dog, keeping his eyes fixed on the cars approaching in four or five lanes in front of him. Several other officers watch him, watch the traffic, ensure his safety and that of the animal.

This is D.H., an officer tells the pilgrim, known as one of the top drug-detectors on the job. Even before the dogs begin their nose work on a vehicle, they need to be pointed toward a car, and it's D.H. who shows them the way.

Wow, wow, wow! it's Salem, a golden retriever working this time, yeah, hey, go on, go on!

Salem tries to shove her muzzle up under the bumper of a new white Honda.

Some weeks they think we're looking for muddy cars so they clean up every car they send through with a load, one of the Customs men says to me as we tag along behind the rambunctious dog. Next week it's all mud and sloppy stuff in the trunk.

Hey, hey, hey!

The dog turns away from the Honda and heads toward an old black van with California plates.

That's the one, D.H. mutters to the inspector coming up along behind him, as if he had been watching for this one vehicle.

Watch, someone says to the pilgrim.

All around, drivers watch from cars sitting in the numerous lanes. Some of them will be seeing it for the first time, the dog tearing with her paws at the metal, saying with every canine gesture, It's here! it's here! they've got some here!

D.H. goes around to the driver's side of the car, asks the driver to step out. Within seconds, he and another inspector have slapped handcuffs on the man and they're leading him alongside cars toward the booths, past the booths, toward Secondary.

That didn't take long, did it?

The pilgrim shakes his head as they follow the car, with an inspector now behind the wheel, past the booths and into Secondary. The driver has already been taken inside. Dog and inspectors go over the car, this time with even greater concentration.

And a mood something like glee.

Yeah, yeah! go get it, go get it!

And the inspectors rush to the vehicle, watching the dog, and then tearing apart the rear bumper with a crowbar.

Where is it?

Do you see it?

I can smell it!

You can? the pilgrim wonders about that. He smells only car exhaust and sweat and dog.

You know, I got a feeling, the inspector says.

Suddenly a shout goes up.

There it is! there it is!

The inspector with the crowbar reaches in beneath the bent metal and yanks out a package wrapped in plastic.

Meth! someone's voice goes up.

Meth!

Oh, some biker gang out in Canoga Park is going to be pissed at us!

But they still have to test it. The inspector calls for a test kit. Someone trots into the office to fetch one. Meanwhile they go over the rest of the car. The glove box. The area behind the steering wheel. Under the wipers.

Other K-9 handlers race over with their dogs, letting these animals get a whiff of the drug, and whooping and hollering when they point to it. Whoomp! a slap with a rolled up towel, and then the dog gets to keep the towel in his jaws. Oh, happy day! a play day! another find!

(*Interlude, New Generation*:

Ten years ago, raven-haired, glistening eyed A.N. was a sixteen-year-old student from Montgomery High School, her father from Juarez, her mother from Mexico City, and one night, while she was a passenger in a car coming back through the San Ysidro Port of Entry after an evening of visiting with relatives in Tijuana, where her father had owned a dance hall for several decades, the driver was ordered by the inspector to pull into Secondary. A.N. got out of the car and watched while a search of the vehicle ensued, intrigued by the procedures. She asked the Customs inspector how he got his job, and he talked a bit with her and then called over a supervisor. That's how she found out about the Explorer Program, the non-profit support organization that introduces young students to the work at the port of entry. She joined the Explorers and after graduating from Montgomery took a job as a student aid at the downtown headquarters of the Customs Service. She took courses at Southwestern College and then completed her bachelor's degree at San Diego State, working full time for Customs during the summers. In 1995 she applied for a job as a Customs inspector and was hired, training for the post at the Customs camp in Georgia, graduating on Valentine's Day 1996, and, as a G-5, taking her post at the San Diego/Tijuana border. Three weeks of supervised training and she was on her own. It was scary to work on my own, especially on the midnight shift, she says. The older generation of (mostly) male inspectors helped her along.

I was everybody's little girl, she says. Men and women get along here. Everybody tries to help you, and lends a hand if you need it. It's so dangerous out here that we have to get along.

But don't get in this little girl's way, since she packs the standard issue 9 mm. Smith & Wesson and scores between 147 and 149 out of 150 on the firing range, and she's required to qualify several times a year. Now she usually works fifty-six hours a week, taking advantage of the frequent opportunities for overtime. In her late teens and early twenties, she used to party a lot in Tijuana, she says. But now, after participating in so many drug seizures, she has put her partying aside. In her spare time she reads and plays volleyball in the YMCA league, baseball in summer, then back to volleyball. She also enjoys deep-sea fishing. A.N. plans to stay with the Customs Service, in a few years perhaps transferring up to the Canadian border.)

11:00 p.m. Out in pre-primary again. The cars have backed up. Nearly fourteen lanes open now. The after-dinner crowd wants to get home to San Diego. But this is a good time, or so smugglers think, to blend their carriers in with the Saturday night crowd, so things go a bit slowly.

That's the thing, a Customs inspector says to me as we roam in the lanes behind the dog. The paradox.

Paradox?

That's right. Paradox. Between facilitation and interdiction. We're supposed to be catching the drugs and we're also supposed to be moving people through at a reasonable rate. We can't do both things and do them well.

Wow! hey! good! that's a girl!

Another find by the K-9s!

Driver steps out of car, cuffed, hustled off to the building. Everybody follows car in to Secondary.

Dogs, men, women swarm over the vehicle.

Hey! that's it! get it, get it, get it!

It's an INS dog this time, and it leaps into the car, digging, digging, digging at the rear seat.

The inspectors yank up the seat, revealing a shallow compartment where an old man and a young boy lay huddled, like fetuses, like corpses. Illegals! They look as though they've traveled here from another dimension, almost as though their very bodies are less substantial than those around them. Blank looks on their faces. Confusion.

Despair.

(The pilgrim imagines that it must have been this look on the faces of Jews trying to steal across the border out of Germany, or out of Vichy France into Spain. Or Tutsis moving across from Rwanda to Burundi. Cambodians. Vietnamese. This is not the look of the Greenhorn, the pilgrim's father stepping off the boat in San Francisco or his grandparents passing through Ellis Island, blinking at the first light in America after long journeys over water. In their eyes, you could have seen hope and perhaps even amazement behind the fatigue. Look at these people and you see nothing but desperation.)

Busy Saturday night in Fortress America! Leaning our shoulders to the door to keep out unwanted guests.

There's an even greater paradox in that, the pilgrim thinks to himself, quietly, trying to keep his opinions from weighing his eyes shut.

(*Interlude with Document, continued*:

4. *Complexity:*

    Incumbent performs inspection duties in compliance with certain federal statutes, and in accordance with established policies and procedures. As necessary, incumbent conducts intensive and detailed interrogations which are prompted by applicants for false entry to the United States who are suspected of: 1) alien smuggling; 2) false claims to United States citizenship; 3) presenting fraudulently obtained documents of others; 4) presenting altered or counterfeit documents; 5) attempting to enter by scheme or devious means; 6) terrorist activity; 7) smuggling of illegal drugs and/or other contraband. Referrals for exclusion hearing must be accurate, concise, and firmly rooted in law. May be called upon to use proper and safe law enforcement techniques in the above cases, including arrest and detention of persons involved. Adjudicates a wide variety of applications and petitions for benefits under the Immigration and Nationality Act, including cases involving novel and complex application of law and regulation.

5. *Scope and effect:*

    The purpose of the position is to properly categorize and admit United States citizens and entitled aliens into the United States. Prompt and efficient performance of duties facilitates legal entry, while denying entry to those not authorized to enter the United States under the exclusion laws (terrorists, narcotic traffickers, etc.).

6. *Personal contacts:*

    Contacts are with people seeking admittance into the United States (and at times, with their representatives), immediate co-workers, and as needed, with personnel from other agencies, foreign governments, and members of the general public.

7. *Purpose of contacts:*
   Purpose of contacts is to obtain information necessary to determine admissibility of people (or goods, where applicable) into the United States.

8. *Physical demands:*
   Position requires moderate to arduous physical exertion involving long periods of standing, walking, the climbing of scaffolds and ladders, including "Jacobs" ladders, use of firearms, and exposure to inclement weather. Extended work hours (more than eight hours a day) are experienced. The lifting and carrying of materials (i.e., "boarding bag") is required to perform the duties of the position. May be required to use physical force to arrest and detain persons as deemed appropriate by Service regulations. Must be prepared to defend self and others against physical attack, resorting to the use of firearms if warranted by the circumstances (self-defense, defense of another officer, or an innocent third party).

9. *Work environment:*
   Work may be performed at one or more of the following sites: border port of entry, seaport, air, or railway. Work is performed both indoors and outdoors. Incumbent may be exposed to inclement weather while working outdoors and shift work.

10. *Other significant factors:*
    Incumbent is required to carry a firearm and be proficient in the use thereof.)

Midnight, on the line.

It can get dangerous out here, says the INS inspector. He's tall, lanky dark-haired, with sharp sculptured high cheekbones that speak of Mexican Indian genes. He signals the next car to move forward. We get about one shooting a year out here. Mexican guy came through the line last year, pulled his car up, didn't say a word, just started firing at the inspector. And the inspector fired back as the car pulled away, and everybody ran up and drew down on this car and started shooting and about a quarter of a mile up the road the guy gave it up, just died there behind the wheel, full of bullet holes. We're good, you know. We got to qualify regularly. Me, last time on the pistol range I was one forty-seven out of one fifty. Not bad. Oh, there was another time out here, a couple of years ago, I wasn't here but I heard about it, a guy came through and tossed a bottle of acid, sulphuric acid or maybe lye? into the booth, trying to blow it up, like with a Molotov cocktail, or maybe it was a Molotov cocktail, anyway, just goes to show you that it can be a battlefield out here. And Saturday night, it gets even crazier than usual, too. All the partyers coming back from TJ. The Americans are the most obnoxious. (Next car. Single driver. Old man.) You ask them their citizenship and they don't even know what you're talking about. Idaho, they say. Kentucky. They don't think how their state has something to do with the country. U.S. That's all they have to say. (Next car. Man and a woman on their way, they say, to Los Angeles. They have the proper papers. Walks around the car, tapping at the side of it with his flashlight.) Magic words. U.S. You wave them through. Of course, they have to say it just right. You can hear the way they say it. Say it to yourself. U.S. Hear the special American accent. A kind of voice. (Next car pulls up. Five girls. Partying in TJ. They flirt a little, giggle a little, travel on.) Something about Americans. Of course, I think American. Got family in Mexico, some in Tijuana, some over near Mexicali. I was born here. Gives me an edge with most of the people coming through this port of entry. (Van pulls up. Takes the driver's identity card. He takes a full half-minute walking around the vehicle, lowering himself beneath the rear bumper, shining his light up into the undercarriage. Full half-minute, which to a driver who knows his car is loaded with bricks of marijuana or meth or packets of cocaine might seem a bit longer. He hands the card back, waves the driver on into the United States.)

I know the moves, the Mexican moves. They can't fool me. Sometimes, they can run a game on the non-Mexican inspectors, but not on me. It's a way of looking, it's a way of moving, it's a way of saying. Every country has it. I know the looking and the moving and the saying of both the U.S. and Mexico. Helps me on the job. (Car moves up, driver's nervous, jugular twitching, won't look the inspector in the eye. This one goes to Secondary.) I'm not one of them, but I know how they think. It's like, being from a different generation. I'm not my parents, but I know how they think. I'm not from Mexico, but I know how they think. (A car pulls up. Old woman, small child. Child's papers look strange to the INS man. He sends them to Secondary.) Yes, and the pilgrim is thinking, how much like himself and the older generation, and how much like himself and the people he grew up with, to know someone but be not of them, often the source of existential estrangement, but in this case, with respect to nationality, a distinction that makes for a real difference, to be Irish American and dealing with Irish immigrants, or Jewish and dealing with Jewish immigrants, Italian and so on, imagine if our country of immigrants shared borders with Ireland and Italy and Israel and Germany and England and Belgium and France and Spain and India and Pakistan and Serbia and Nigeria and Argentina and Kenya and South Africa and Sweden…And tens of thousands of aliens from these nations came up to the line every day, and who would know them better than their cousins and nephews and nieces who were born in the United States of that particular lineage?

Would you not be more strict with those you knew than with those you didn't, versed in their canniness and guile as well as their charm and intelligence? Some hard-nosed interrogator might put the old divided loyalty argument out on the table, to ask if a man like this might be moved beyond the usual sympathy for a special case and skirt the rules for someone of his old kin. It's an argument that Japanese Americans met during World War II, and were interned for. No benefit of the doubt given to them. It's an argument that American Jews have faced ever since the advent of the State of Israel. And while every now and then we've seen someone in a position of trust on our side cross over the line to give special attention to someone on the other side, they have been few in number. Think of all the Japanese Americans who fought in World War II. Think of the German American and Italian American boys who died in the European theater. Think of all these Mexican American inspectors on the line, giving this job their above and beyond.

I moved here from Calexico where I was working at the port there, the inspector says. Couple years on the job. But things began to happen. I'd be in Mexicali on the other side and people would recognize me. Such a small place there, you know. And then some people said some things to my relatives in Calexico. Not to me directly, but to some family members. I figured it was time for me to leave. So I put in for a transfer. (Waves up a car, checks it over, passes it through.)

Exhaust boils up, mixing a strange brew in the cool of the night air, all the noise of the fans and the engines, loud music from car radios, the telephones that ring now and then in the booths, every now and then the tap of a horn drifting over from far back toward the "dip" where drivers wait for what they take to be an endless time, click of the keys on the computer keyboards in the booths. Everything but human speech. No noise of language out here in Primary, among the rows of cars leading to the inspection booths.

All roads in western Mexico lead to this crossing, this great funneling of travelers and families and smugglers and heroes and gangsters and children and fathers and mothers and cousins and sisters and brothers, and all roads along the western edge of the United States funnel down to this great crossing—yes, yes, the pilgrim knows about the crossing at Otay Mesa, but here at San Ysidro is the great crossing point, nexus of countries, nexus of cultures, nexus of visions, nexus of borderlands between first world and third, between Old world and New, ancient and modern, for some even the interface between life and death, past and future, the narrow point where all good and bad and old and young and healthy and sick and sighted and blind and stupid and genius and everything in between all come together.

Border time: all sorts of visions rise up out of the trembling line, the imaginary three-thousand-mile demarcation that Carlos Fuentes has called "the crystal frontier," a place of transformations and hallucinations. Step right up to it and you have to answer to yourself on some important issues. Do you believe we should have an open border? Just let people come and go as they please? A writer in a local monthly has utopian dreams of blending the cities of San Diego and Tijuana. "American prosperity will slither south and fix some of Baja's problems and Mexican *joie de vivre* will slither north and spice up white-bread San Diego. I don't think anything very serious will happen if you just take the damned thing down..."

Slither is probably the right word. Open the gates and up from the South will travel a number of rough beasts, the pilgrim muses.

Given the desperate drug addiction of millions of North Americans, the future with an open border could promise a national narcotic orgy beyond our imaginings, or at least something within the realm of the visions of William Burroughs. As for a border wide-open to immigrants from around the world, only the radical free-market economists might make predictions about what that would do to the way we live and earn and spend now. Opening the border would be a Faustian gesture, to say that we accept everything and everyone that might come our way—the picture lends itself to science fiction as well as medieval tragedy. Boat upon boat of the hungry and the ambitious from all over the planet, trainloads, carloads, truckloads of dreamers without body fat, carrying within their loins and wombs the makings of an America no present residents, whether of four generations U.S. born, or newly naturalized citizens, would welcome. Picture it then: the United States, already the greatest political experiment in modern history, lending itself to become whatever it might evolve to, its arms open wide to whomever and whatever seeks us out as home. That would be known as the boldest gesture any nation had ever made. Who knows what the archaeologists of the future would piece together from the remains of a nation that made such a policy?

(Interlude with Documents:

U.S. Immigration Service, San Ysidro Port of Entry, Incident Report/ Seizure Report. From:——. Title: Immigration. Day: Saturday. Date:—— Year: 1998. Make: Ford. Model: Sedan. Color: Blue. License:——. State: Ca. **Note: This form must be executed and turned in to the office of the Area Port Director no later than the end of your assigned shift on the date of the occurrence of the incident/seizure.

Narrative (use additional sheet if necessary): On January 23,

1998, subject——, a Mexican citizen, applied for entry into the United States from Mexico as the driver of above mentioned vehicle via the San Ysidro Port of Entry. I referred into vehicle Secondary office for a form I-94 in order for him to travel to Los Angeles. While he was in Secondary, I was later informed by the U.S. Customs Service, it was found that the vehicle contained 1.6 lbs. of field-tested positive marijuana… [officer's signature. shift supervisor's signature])

At Pedestrian Inspection: 1:00 a.m. The pilgrim wanders across the exit lanes on the east side of the Secondary Inspection area toward the building that houses the pedestrian inspection lanes. But then he hears the by-now familiar sound of inspectors on the run.

Where are they going?

Over to the roadway, someone calls back over her shoulder. There's an operation going on.

The pilgrim hurries along behind them, crossing back through Secondary and over the exit lanes on the west side of the port and over the median to where a half dozen police cars have blocked the southbound road, except for the farthest lane, checking cars just as they slow down for the approach to the Mexican entry booths.

There's a light drizzle, the water forming coronas around the headlamps of the cars. Bright lamps overhead illuminating the entrance to the Mexican inspection lanes. Streams of people move from the parking lot on the far side of the road up onto the overhead crosswalk that will take them into Mexico. It's like a stadium just before a game, or a stadium just after the final whistle is blown. Honking horns make a haphazard chorus as cars slow down for the impromptu pre-border checkpoint. Inspectors call to one another for assistance over the noise of the cars.

Walking back and forth on the side of the road is a tall blond man in a rain slicker with PAROLE OFFICER in large yellow

letters on the back. Spying the pilgrim he comes over and asks
for ID.

The pilgrim explains what he's doing here. The parole officer
outlines the purpose of the checkpoint, a joint operation of
Customs and various state and local law enforcement agencies,
which culls underage drivers heading across to Mexico to drink,
felons on the run (or felons heading across the border for a night
on the town), money launderers, illegal weapons, drugs.

Not much doing during the next half hour, as the pilgrim feels
the drizzle soak into his skull, except a bunch of gang kids sitting
on the curb waiting for the inspectors to finish looking over their
vehicles. The pilgrim casts his mind back up the long lines of
traffic, imagining what the drivers a mile or two back along the
backup must be thinking, most of them just annoyed, a few of them
wondering, a handful rather fearful. This is security and crime
prevention in America on the verge of the new century, where the
people the police are trying to protect must suffer a few delays.

Some kid goes drinking, the parole officer is saying, over in
Tijuana, comes back driving drunk, rear-ends some innocent
person on his way to work. The party ends in tragedy. We're
trying to prevent that.

Hey, officer, says one of the kids on the curb. He's in a tee-
shirt, head shaved, looking like somebody who wants to do battle,
probably hungering for an evening on the town in TJ.

Just a few minutes more, sir, the parole officer says to him.

We're gonna be late to be early, the kids says. His friends laugh.
The drizzle stops. The horns sound. The officers roam from car to
car, making their inspections.

A car came out of Mexico one time, an inspector sidles up to
me and begins to tell me a story, the guy was shooting as he came
through, and he jogged left here into this lane and he's racing

north toward the city in these southbound lanes, and everybody's running after the car, shooting at him.

The pilgrim recalls having heard this story earlier in the evening, one of the legends of the port of entry. The wrong-way driver. Everybody shooting.

He didn't make it a hundred yards up the road, the pilgrim says. Right, the inspector says. That's exactly right.

(**Interlude with Lawman**:

Sixth floor of the Federal Building downtown, a view west over the port, across Coronado, to Point Loma and the Pacific sky beyond. In striped shirt, plain tie, neat trousers, ankle-top leather boots, Alan Bersin [still in his incarnation as U.S. Attorney for Southern California] reminds the pilgrim of his lifelong friend Robert Pinsky, currently Poet Laureate of the United States. There's a clarity to the lawman's speech that's pushed along by certainty, like a sailboat on the edge of a steady blow. And a toughness to his stance born of early days of growing up in Brooklyn and playing football at Harvard that adds starch to the stance of the former Rhodes Scholar, Yale Law graduate, old pal of the President and First Lady. In other words, the pilgrim immediately gets the impression that as wily and as dangerous as are the drug families of Mexico they have met their match in this stand-up prosecutor and intellectual. Here is a man who is perhaps as close to becoming a poet of law enforcement as he is to making the picture of an old-fashioned western marshal.

As he makes clear in his essay, "El Tercer País: Reinventing the U.S./Mexico Border," from the May 1996 Stanford Law Review, Bersin doesn't just have policies, he has ideas. In the essay, he writes of transforming regional transborder policies as a way of bringing order to the traditionally chaotic territory where one country faces the other, sometimes in awe, sometimes in dismay, and he recommends binational congeries made up of regional businessmen, politicians, and law enforcement people to recommend policy for the trans-national region San Diego and Tijuana have the potential to become.

"There's a paradigm-shift that's happened at the border," Bersin says, offering impressive statistics to point up the decline in crime, particularly car theft and burglaries on the southern San Diego side of the border line since the inception of Gatekeeper. (A 48 percent decline in auto theft, 30 percent decline in burglaries...) His guide in this is the so-called broken-window theory of law enforcement, enforcement that practices zero tolerance.

Park a car on the street and it may sit for weeks untouched. Break one window, and the vehicle becomes a target for all sorts of rascals and scavengers and thieves. Within a few days you'll see more damage, and then major theft of various parts. The notion is—and we have seen this work in New York City and other large urban areas—that if you do not enforce the legal code down to its dotted i's and crossed t's, you induce a lack of respect for all the laws.

But Bersin, about to leave this office for a career in education, is a man with a vision, a type ordinarily considered quite dangerous among the court house crowd. With the help of the San Diego Dialogue, a binational group of business and political leaders, his goal has been to create political and social mechanisms to ensure that the moral climate of these two overlapping cities divided down the middle by the national border will remain beneficial to all citizens on both sides of the line.

If the men and women at the port of entry could hear him speak, they would redouble their efforts at making a real dialectic out of interdiction and facilitation. If the dogs could hear him and understand, they would sniff twice as hard for contraband. This lawman has worked as hard as anyone to make policies that will outlast his own tenure.)

1:30 a.m.—The stories that keep people going on this job, the continual search for a load of drugs, for the cache of human cargo stashed away under seats or in trunks.

Once, an inspector says, we opened the hood of this car, and you could see that the space alongside the engine block was too small, and we pried open this compartment and there were two children, one on each side of the engine block, little kids, nearly dead from the fumes.

Sirens whine as a CHP car pulls over a vehicle in the far lane. The pilgrim's aching head is getting soaked.

(*Interlude with the Border Patrol:*

Out in the dark to the west of the port of entry, they're riding in their four-by-fours, moving along wet, rough Monument Road, past a few small family ranches and some other houses, into the weird territory along the line just north of the Ensenada Highway, where new steel fencing has made it almost impossible for anyone to make it beyond about a hundred yards into U.S. territory. Every night, they're out there, constantly changing position, then hunkering behind the wheels of their vehicles, lights out, watching the dark for movement.

It's wet out tonight, R.S., the agent, says to the pilgrim. So people will be on the move. They think we won't want to get out there and chase them in the rain and the mud.

Up and over thick muddy trails, and suddenly the lights of the vehicle are reflecting off the embankment directly at the side of the highway. The pilgrim has seen this place before, in tapes taken not so many years ago, when hundreds of people jumped down onto the American side and started running past the helpless border patrolmen. He has also read Joseph Wambaugh's Lines and Shadows, *a nonfiction narrative about the special San Diego Police Department squad that in the late*

1970s patrolled the border line in order to prevent crime against illegals by scavengers on both sides of the mostly symbolic fence between the United States and Mexico.

"So the task force assembled across the canyons and chose their observation points, from which they would support each other, observe crimes, arrest bandits, and corral victims. And they would look at one another in wonder when hundreds of other aliens suddenly materialized in the dusk. Human beings of all ages would rise up as though from the earth itself. People who had been invisible—resting, sleeping, eating, praying. Up from the mesquite and the rocks and the skeletal oaks. They would simply rise up!...And then it was dark. Just like that...The hills began to move. The masses began to surge northward on their journeys to the land of plenty..."

Now, there's no one here.

There was a campfire over there the other night, R.S. says, pointing to a spot just beyond the wall. No one there now. Since 1994, when Operation Gatekeeper went into effect, we've reduced border jumpers in this area, the most popular route for illegal immigration to the United States, down almost to zero. We've reached the lowest rate of apprehensions in seventeen years.

Yes, the pilgrim thinks to himself, remembering some statistics he saw before coming out for his night ride along the border line. The government has increased spending for INS about 53 percent since 1993 and by the end of 1998 will have seven thousand border patrol agents on the job, twice as many as in 1993. John Williams, former head of the San Ysidro Port of Entry, and one of the godfathers of Gatekeeper, can look south from his new desk at the INS headquarters in Laguna Niguel, and be pleased.

On the Mexican side of the big drainage slough that parallels the border for a few thousand yards, we see figures moving, and they could be kids playing or they could be adults trying to figure out how to cross over to our side.

A Border Patrol vehicle sits waiting for one or more of them to make a decisive move.

But for most of the time the only signs of life we see are the other Border Patrol officers sitting behind their steering wheels. Some of them don't want to talk to the pilgrim, refusing to put themselves in jeopardy. They have been fired on from the Mexican side of the border. They have been threatened. They don't want their names in the paper.

And then the pilgrim meets a charming, black, former Transit Department (read, Subway) cop from Brooklyn, who loves the job and talks awhile about the importance of it, as he sees it, leaning way out of the vehicle to make a point with flailing hands.

It's great work, he says. Tedious sometimes, but you always think about your mission and that keeps you going.

The pilgrim nods, smiles at the guy, and can almost hear his inner voice, explaining his mission to himself. You know, everybody, no matter who he is and what he believes, he'd protect their family and his household, right? That's what I see I'm doing. I'm protecting the house. I'm guarding the doorway of the American house!)

1:45 a.m. The pilgrim heads back through Secondary where groups of inspectors gather at the rotation sheet, dogs roam up the pavement at the end of short leads. It's dinnertime for those with appetites. Someone goes out to Taco Bell with an order for a number of inspectors. Two automobile searches later, and the food arrives. In the main building, ground floor, a small lunchroom, with tables, chairs, soda machines, the pilgrim sits down with an uncustomary plate before him. (He's given up meat some years ago.) Here most of the inspectors eat fast food every day and night. There's only thirty minutes to eat. Fast is necessary.

Though one man in his early thirties sits across from the pilgrim, chewing on barbecued chicken and eating salad and fruit from small plastic containers.

From home? the pilgrim asks.

The inspector nods.

A lot of people work here don't have anybody at home to make them dinner, he says. I'm lucky.

The pilgrim chews on his unnameable taco and agrees.

A middle-aged female inspector comes into the room and sits with a container of coffee on the table before her, and a novel in front of her eyes.

John Grisham.

Enjoying it? the pilgrim inquires.

I like to read, the inspector says, shifting the book slightly in front of her. If there's a really good book, we pass it around.

The pilgrim remembers his nights in the booth on the New Jersey Turnpike, the still hours between late night and false dawn when only a few cars might approach the gate, when he read Proust and Thomas Wolfe, lost in the seemingly endless pages of amazing prose rolling past his eyes beneath the odd illumination of the toll plaza lamps. (Reading is the true hallucinatory experience, a high that rivals any drug, and dictators have known this, making books contraband from time to time in the worst times of the modern world. And wasn't it only about seventy years ago that Customs inspectors confiscated copies of *Ulysses* at the New York port of entry? and copies of the books of Henry Miller as recently as forty years ago?)

The pilgrim promises to send the woman a copy of one of his own books, apologizing to her—and to himself, he supposes— because they're not John Grisham and they aren't Proust, either. Then he washes down the remaining shreds of his taco with an overly sweet lemony soft drink and returns to Secondary.

He nods to some Customs officers he's seen earlier, then crosses the exit lanes and enters the Pedestrian building. There he meets W.C., a Customs inspector and former navy veteran. W.C. explains the intricate crossing and recrossing of Customs and INS inspectors on the job. We supplement each other, complement each other. They're mainly watching for fake documents, for imposters, felons on the loose, and we're looking for drugs and contraband.

It's an important job, W.C. says. X thousands of people cross here on foot every day, going to work in the morning, coming home at night, coming across to shop, going over to TJ to shop and eat. And it's challenging. I wake up every morning and can't wait to put on my uniform and go to work.

We watch as a busload of tourists enter the building, checked in by an INS inspector at the door, and then funnel along the side of the building to the exit where their bus will meet them, having been checked over by Customs inspectors.

We've found big loads in buses, W.C. says. So we have to keep an eye on them.

Adults and children, Italian tourists, shuffle along to meet their bus. One of them wanders through the wrong turnstile. An INS inspector raises his voice in annoyance, pointing the way back toward the exit for the bus.

W.C. says, The only problem I have with this job is watching some of the other people behave like that. Not showing courtesy to the people coming across. It hurts me to see that. But otherwise, it's the best job in the world.

Another Customs inspector who was listening while we spoke steps up and adds this to our conversation: there's another problem. You probably heard about it already. Facilitation opposed to interdiction?

The pilgrim nods, yes, he's heard.

The INS folks, this man says, they just want to move people along.

It's their supervisors, we hear it from ours, they hear it probably more from theirs. They set the pace.

Yeah, well, if we had time, we'd get all the drugs. Right now, what do we get, 10 percent of the stuff moving through here?

The other inspector shrugs. Nobody really knows. They say 10 percent. But it could be 1 percent, it could be 20 percent.

*(**Interlude, Undercover**—*

Earlier in the week while standing at the pedestrian crossing, the pilgrim noticed a tall, blond-haired fellow in jeans and windbreaker who sidled up to the inspection turnstiles and watched intently as people came through.

He's S.R., an INS agent in plainclothes, on the tail end of an undercover operation to track smugglers of illegals. We exchange a few words, and the pilgrim walks out the door with him, shadowing the shadower of a twenty-five-year-old Mexican man in a leather jacket who has just passed through Immigration. Out onto the street, into the crowd, along the pavement, across the street, past a parking lot, and then into the Burger King. We hurry along, trying to look nonchalant and move quickly at the same time. Seven other agents in plainclothes dot the landscape, but the pilgrim's moving too fast to be able to spot them all. Into the restaurant where the pilgrim buys a cup of coffee for the agent and an orange juice for himself. There's no time to sip, as the apparent fugitive leaves the restaurant and heads back toward the trolley stop.

Going to ride the trolley to town with me? the agent asks.

The pilgrim hesitates, torn between the lure of going out on an undercover operation and the duty of remaining at the port of entry to keep up his watch.

But then the plan falls apart as the man in the leather jacket decides not to take the trolley, and the agent takes off after him as the pilgrim turns back toward the entrance to the pedestrian crossing.)

2:00 a.m. G.S. enters the building. He's on his second shift, working here at Pedestrian as a supervisor. You're going to see quite a show tonight, he tells the pilgrim. Saturday night, in a little while, they're all going to start coming back across, a lot of kids from San Diego who've gone over to get drunk. It's quite a sight.

(*Interlude, Sierra Club argues About Closing the Door*—

"In the next few weeks, the half million members of the Sierra Club will vote to set the club's policy on the issue of immigration...the debate, which has already been spirited, represents an invaluable chance to raise the issue of how many people this country can and should contain...If we're not willing to reduce the size of our families or the size of our sport utility vehicles, then cutting immigration is piggish scapegoating; it may save some of our landscape, but at the price of our national soul..." Bill McKibben, New York Times, March 9, 1998)

2:15 a.m. INS inspectors converge on a thin, dazed brown-skinned boy of about seventeen as he walks through the turnstile. He's carrying no luggage, says to them when they ask where he's going,
"Sacraclemente…"
"Where?"
"Sacraclemente…"
The inspectors hustle him off to the INS office at the far corner of the building. The pilgrim follows along to see him place his fingerprint in the new "Ident" system reader and have his photograph taken. An inspector tells him to take a seat on the bench along the wall. The computer searches for a match for the fingerprint. If he has tried to cross the border before and been

apprehended, the machine should discover this. (The Ident system is one of the results of the more than one *billion* dollar budget increase for automation and technology that INS has seen since 1995. Since 1990, the INS budget has increased by 223 percent, from $1.176 *billion* to $3,799 *billion* dollars!)

A commotion outside the office catches the pilgrim's attention, and he wanders back outside to see a long line of revelers suddenly swelling the hall. It's as if every Saturday night is New Year's Eve here at the Pedestrian crossing, with shouts and songs and yelps and whoops coming from the staggering crowd of partyers returning from their night in TJ.

Here's a group of girls in their mid to late teens, dressed to twist and shout, two of them holding up a friend in the middle who seems on the verge of alcohol poisoning.

Here's a gaggle of servicemen, several of them nearly brought to their knees from drink, struggling to stand upright as they lurch up to the INS inspector at the turnstile.

It's like that George Jones song, an inspector says, where he sings how his bloodstream's become a distillery?

Another inspector watches the crowd with cold eyes.

Not to mention what else they got in their bloodstreams, he says.

G.S. comes up to the pilgrim and says, They're somebody's children, and look at them. You think their folks know where they are right now? I doubt it. He watches, watches, like a hawk on a wire, studying the landscape below.

Telephone rings. G.S. answers it. I'm heading back over to Secondary for a few minutes, he says. Some pharmaceuticals they need some advice about.

He's our pharmaceuticals guy, a young clean-shaven Customs inspector says to the pilgrim. If it's something made in Mexico that can't come into the United States, he's the one who knows about it. He's been training Europeans about how to do that kind of work. Nice specialty.

The pilgrim listens and watches the line, trying to inhabit the spirit of the hour, watching faces for some revelatory quiver, watching hands that might shake out of fear of discovery.

Where're you from? a burly INS inspector behind the desk at the center turnstile says to a group of ruddy-faced, crew-cut tourists.

U.S., one says.

U.S. of A., another says.

America, a third says.

He passes them along.

He studies documents, he looks people in the eye. Now and then takes someone's hand and studies the prints on their forefingers, comparing them to the prints on their identity cards.

Where're you from?

Alabama.

Country? the inspector says.

Alabama.

Where's that? the inspector asks.

The sailor raises his voice.

Where's Alabama?

The inspector at the pilgrim's shoulder says, I hate it when they do that.

Which one? the pilgrim says.

When the INS guy gives them a hard time. So the guy says Alabama instead of the U.S. Big deal.

A female sailor behind the Alabamian says something to the INS inspector at the turnstile.

What? the inspector says. Heads turn at his raised voice.

Why are you giving us such a hard time? the woman says.

All right, the inspector says, folding his arms across his chest, as if to say, Want to stay in Mexico? Fine with me.

I wish he wouldn't do that, the inspector at the pilgrim's side says. But you know it's the law, even if you're a citizen, once you leave the country, you've got no automatic right to come back in. But this guy, he's just fooling with them.

The woman shouts at the inspector, a loud noise, but her words are garbled.

Whoa! a shore patrolman, on duty all night to watch for trouble among returning seamen, rushes over to the turnstile and the INS inspector jerks his thumb toward the sailors. The noise rises, the line lengthens behind the turnstile until several other INS inspectors open up new lanes and take the overflow. The INS man gestures to the sailors to pass. The shore patrolman takes them aside just on this side of the turnstiles. He speaks to them in low quick sentences about alcohol and about courtesy. The female sailor jerks herself around and stalks back to the angry inspector.

I'm sorry, she spits out at him.

He shrugs and goes back to his line of waiting pilgrims.

A Customs inspector standing just in front of another turnstile suddenly surges forward, calling to a blond hulk of a fellow, clearly American by his walk and his clothing, who has just crossed over the line.

Yes, sir? the fellow says.

The inspector asks him to step up to the long table nearby and open his suitcase.

Another inspector watches at the pilgrim's shoulder.

What's his problem? the pilgrim asks.

This guy is stoned, high on something or other.

The blond fellow talks a mile a minute, fussing with the clothing in his suitcase, emptying his pockets for the inspector.

Nothing illegal in hand.

Out of a crowd of foreign tourists just disembarked from a tour bus, a man steps over. In Germany, we destroyed our wall. You should be ashamed, you keep this wall up.

The inspector shrugs, as if a passing bird has deposited guano on his shoulder. He searches through the suitcase, takes the young man inside, while G.S. runs a check on him in the computer. A few minutes later, they release him.

Whatever he took tonight, it's in his bloodstream, not his suitcase, G.S. says.

(*Interlude,* **Letter to the** New York Times, *March 13, 1998—*

"*The headline on the article by Bill McKibben says it all ('Immigrants Aren't the Problem, We Are,' Op-Ed, March 9). With well over a million immigrants coming in every year, we will nearly double our population by 2050. How will we be able to deliver necessary infrastructure like water, sewage disposal, transportation, food, and police and fire protection to twice as many people when we are barely able to cope in many areas of the country now?...This argument has nothing to do with nativism, racism, or any other 'ism.' In the nineteenth and early twentieth centuries, we needed low-skill immigrants to fuel the Industrial Revolution. Today, immigrants crowd our schools, hospitals, and prisons. We must weigh self-interest in decisions on immigration.*" *Byron Slater. San Diego, March 9, 1998*)

2:30 a.m. Hundreds more pour through the turnstiles after their late night on the town in TJ. The pilgrim remembers a line of

Dante's, in the *Inferno*, after seeing the vast number of souls crossing the border from the land of the living into the outlying reaches of Hell. "I never knew that Death had undone so many..."

They keep coming, singing, chanting, yipping, snorting, many more of them dragged along by friends, made into near corpses from drink on the other side. Tall ones, short ones, pretty girls, their clothing askew, as if they've just been roughed up at a fraternity party, sailors in civilian clothes who appear to have fallen on their faces on the pavement and then jerked upright, like puppets on a string...dark skin, light skin, long hair, short hair, eyes rolling with booze, noses running, hands flapping. The air in the building seems permeated now with the sweet stench of whiskey, as if a weather system of alcohol has settled over the place for the duration.

Behind him, the pilgrim hears a conversation. Two female parole officers, a slender, athletic looking woman in jeans and a denim jacket with an impressive blond permanent and a lithe black woman with close-cropped hair looking as though she might be a literature instructor ready in the wings before a lecture on African American poetry, are discussing their private lives.

A flabby-chested black shore patrolman standing a few yards away calls over to the black woman.

Baby, he says, his high-pitched voice almost a musical whine.

How you doing? she calls back, lapsing into the vernacular.

Doing just fine, the man says.

Mobs flow through the turnstiles, pass between them. He's only got eyes for her. She watches the faces in the crowd.

Baby? he says.

She flicks a smile in his direction, then turns back to the crowd.

Slow, the blond parole officer says.

Uh-huh, she says. Except for him, meaning the shore patrolman.

They keep on talking among themselves. The parole officer whom the pilgrim encountered on the highway operation earlier comes into the building. A Mexican American plainclothes INS agent takes up a stand next to the parole officer, talking about events that occurred earlier in the day.

The rhythm of their voices, of their vigil, reminds the pilgrim of fishermen on the shore.

How's it going?

Okay.

And what's been happening?

This and that.

That and this.

So many loads of marijuana. A load of meth. Found some heroin. Two kids hiding in a compartment built under a van. Fellow walking alongside a van trying to sneak through the line.

And then suddenly they've got a bite. An INS inspector nods and a Customs inspector moves up alongside a tall, husky young man, brown hair, light mustache, wearing a checked wool jacket and jeans, just as he passes through the turnstiles.

Excuse me, sir, but do you mind stepping over here.

Why not, the fellow says, and comes over to the table. The two parole officers converge on him as the Customs inspector asks him to empty his pockets. Everyone notices the thick curlicue of tattoos on his thick forearms that rise up under his jacket sleeves.

The plainclothes INS man begins to question him while the parole officers watch carefully from nearby.

Where you coming from?

The Customs inspector slides an identity card from the man's wallet and hands it to the plainclothes agent.

TJ.

What were you doing there? The agent studies the card, turns it over and studies it again.

You know, the fellow says, eating, drinking.

Now the agent studies the man's face. You bring anything back with you?

No, the fellow says. Just what I ate.

Good food over there, the agent says. This is not a question.

Oh, yeah, the man says.

And good prices, the agent says.

That's when the pilgrim notices that G.S. has come back into the building and taken a stand at the edge of the table.

How long were you in? the agent says.

Seven years, the man says.

Clearly, they're not talking anymore about a visit to Tijuana.

Are you on parole? The blond parole officer steps into the conversation.

The man says, Not on parole. I got a job.

Where do you work? the agent says.

The man tells him.

And you're not on parole? the woman says.

That's right, the man says. I'm finished.

What were you in for? the woman asks him.

I have to talk about it?

Come on inside and we'll talk about it, the agent says, and he motions for the man to walk around to his side of the table and then leads him in to a small room at the front of the hall.

G.S. has already walked into the office at the side of the hall where he taps out a name on the computer.

The pilgrim watches the crowds surge through the turnstiles, listens to the raucous sounds of their early morning passage. Like some performer from a passing circus, a black-garbed border patrolman on a bicycle pedals slowly through the hall and out the side door. A federal policeman, big thick belly proceeding him, waddles toward the turnstiles and then turns and announces to the assembled Customs and INS inspectors, I godda go home. I can't take this no more!

A few inspectors nod, nobody laughs.

G.S. steps out of the office and the parole officers converge on him.

He's on parole, one of them says to the pilgrim a moment later. Served time for murder, in a gang fight when he was seventeen.

He's gone, the woman says. You can't cross over into Mexico if you're on parole.

Back to prison for him.

That's it? the pilgrim says.

That's it, the parole officer says.

The pilgrim doesn't have much time to consider the swiftness of this transition, the fellow coming back from a night of carousing—or who knew what?—in another country just a few feet over the county line and now he's on his way back to prison. Zero tolerance all around is a powerful sight to witness.

3:00 a.m. Approaching that hour of the night, of the early morning, when all things that seem to have happened may happen again without any of the observers believing them to be true. In their beds, all over America, citizens turn in sleep, some without any dreaming witness to their laboring slumber, others seeing endless processions of fears and hopes and lust and mercies coming up to the turnstile, declaring their place of origin, and continuing on through to the other side. Some of these dreamers have come from Guam, some from Guanajuato, some from Lvov, others from Tashkent, Mongolia, Urgench, Dublin, Mombasa, Belfast, Capetown, Irapuato, San Cristóbal de las Casas, Yokohoma, Shanghai, and thousands of villages less hopeful even than these. And these dreamers have children who sleep also at this full hour of the night, and these children have children, so that a full cast of the population of this county, and the state, and the nation made up of all these states swelled with the homesteads of immigrants and the children of immigrants makes up the United States of Helpless Dreamers, citizens in their beds all vulnerable to whatever menace tries to creep upon them in their unawakeful conditions.

Who stands at the door? at the gate? at the turnstile? at the window? keeping watch for intruders at this fragile hour?

3:15 a.m. Listless drunks proceed through the turnstiles, bringing home to America bellies full of digesting food and large quantities of alcohol already rising through their veins to test the blood/brain barrier. While earlier in the night there might have been something of a contest between illegals and inspectors, between smugglers and inspectors, schemes pitted against surveillance, wiliness going against canniness full head on, now there is no contest. Those crossing over have already crossed a line in their minds, if not in their lives: they are prisoners of time, returning to be repatriated to daylight, having lost the battle of the revelry of the night before. One or two of them might make an occasional yelp, but they all move like sheep to be herded, and their crossings are simple and swift.

Where you from?

USA.

Where you headed?

Back to base.

Where you from?

Chula Vista.

Where you headed?

Going home, man, going home.

A K-9 corpsman—a black woman with curly orange hair, looking bulky in her uniform of deep blue—passes through the hall, allowing her dog to sniff at the ankles and the sacks of the stragglers wandering toward the turnstiles.

Yes, baby, she says to the dog. That's a girl, that's a girl.

Another Border Patrolman winds around the hall on his bike.

Where you coming from?

TJ, sure.

Where you going?

Chula Vista.

Where were you born?

U.S. of A.

Where you going?

San Diego.

What'ch you got there in that bag?

Cheese. Cheese and tacos.

Let's take a look.

Okay, okay.

Where you—

Chula—

Born where?

U.S.

Going home or coming from home?

What time is it?

Four in the morning.

Then I don't know, man, I just don't know.

The rhythms of the voices, the slurrings of the night, the suitcases and backpacks and grocery sacks unloaded, sifted through, repacked, odors of food, odors of bodies some perfumed, some unwashed, the heat of men and women and dogs and children, exhaust of automobiles, the roar of fans, the clank of doors. This is what we do, pass back and forth across these lines of demarcation, night and day, year after year, until finally we come to the final port of entry, where we all lay our burdens down and pass, bidden or unbidden, needing no cards of identity to make the ultimate crossing to that undiscovered country just over the frontier from where we have made our marks and mistakes and merriment and madness and good deeds and bad.

Whoa!

A noise rips the texture of the diminishing hour. At first the pilgrim thinks it's a dog handler whose animal has just sniffed out a load of marijuana or some other contraband narcotic. But no, coming through the line is the wife of the driver of the Chevy Silverado all those many hours earlier, struggling to hold her squirming retarded four-year-old, her other two children trailing along behind, towing suitcases behind them.

Her husband in detention, she has been released herself, and now will try to make her way into San Ysidro, to go who knows where.

Oaaah! the retarded girl bellows, writhing so much that she nearly turns head down in her mother's arms and almost falls to the floor. Oaaaah! pure misery! the father arrested, the mother struggling, the child damaged and confused.

Oaaah!

All the inspectors turn toward this pair as the mother passes through the turnstile and stops to adjust the weight of the flailing child.

G.S. steps forward, reaches her quickly, takes the child from the mother and adjusts her in his arms, walking beside the Mexican woman as the fractured family wanders to the exit and trundles off into what is left of the night.

The pilgrim, tired beyond fatigue, makes his own exit, leaving behind the last watches of this port of entry shift, drives north awhile to his bed, closes his eyes, and dreams of endless lines of men, women, children, donkeys, horses, buffalo, sheep, and birds overhead, thick dark clouds of birds, swirling, veering, squawking, honking at the travelers below. It's as if all the rest of the world wants to gain entry to his dream, and there is not enough room, not enough room at all.

Originally published in the San Diego Reader

BORDER SCHOOLING

1—Setting Forth from Bonita

Light knows no fences or perimeters.

It's early Monday morning—Lunes—in winter, just past six, on both sides of the border, and in a small house in Bonita, the family of eleven-year-old Jovanna Venegas is up and about, father José, mother Julia, and Jovanna, a slight, pretty brown-haired girl, getting ready for the school day, both Monday and Lunes. Jovanna dresses in a plaid school jumper and green school sweater and square dark shoes with laces. She eats a skimpy breakfast, a muffin with chocolate milk, while her mother prepares her lunch, a sandwich, a container with carrots, cucumbers, and chiles. Her father wakes to begin his day, nearly thirty years at this business of raising his four girls, of whom Jovanna is the last to live at home. (California home, with its comforts, where the Venegas family moved sixteen years ago from Tijuana after then-president López Portillo nationalized the banks, this California house with its huge, overbearing mortgage!) In a short while, he and Jovanna will be making the ten-minute drive down the 805 to 5 to cross over into Tijuana. Cool early February morning, mist rising off the bay, and to the east, where the sun is just easing its way over the mountains, gold bleeds across the already lightening sky. A bit of a chill in the air when you step outside. But you know that the day will warm up enough to chase the chill away.

And there's the city ahead, straddling the southern hillsides, looking almost as though there were no barrier between this highway and its particular streets. If you have lived there and moved north, you sometimes muse as you drive toward it on what life was like in those days. The old days. When you didn't have to make this drive every day. Still, not a lot of traffic heading south this time of morning. It's the lucky ones who commute south. In the northbound lanes the lines at the San Ysidro border crossing are long. You can imagine the urgency mixed with fatigue, the rush and the holding back in the drivers and passengers in those vehicles. Monday morning rush hour charges the hearts and nervous systems of tens of millions throughout the country, but here, at the border, there's an exquisite layer of torture and exhilaration added to that already blood-pounding mix. Not just to get to work on time, not just to begin the work week, five days, counting this same morning, that lie ahead, with all of their duties and hard labor and passions and rewards and errors and problems and tortures and blindness and insight, hopes and fears. Not just rush hour on a Monday- –Lunes!—but rush hour at the border. To have to cross an international frontier to get to work each day, now that should be placed on a list of ordeals some time to be erased by international tribunal at the U.N.

But for the Venegas family, rolling south each workday, it's just an easy easing of brakes, winding slowly between the concrete barriers on the roadway, and entering their old hometown. José owns a photography studio in a shopping center on Agua Caliente across from the country club, a business he has operated for almost thirty years. But before he goes to his studio, he takes the loop onto the Ensenada highway and drives west on this narrow corridor between the international border fence and the barren hills and ravines immediately to the right and the ramshackle poor neighborhoods of Tijuana just to the left. Up and around the dangerous curve where just as you catch a glimpse of San Diego to the north and the sea directly west the road pitches south toward Ensenada—memorial crosses stand at this curve, a notice that some drivers turned sightseers didn't complete the curve—and at the bottom of the hill you turn off to the right where the exit for Playas comes up quickly. Three minutes later and the car rolls to a stop at the curb next to the upper school of the Colegio Inglés.

Jovanna attends the fifth grade at one of the two buildings that comprise the campus of this private bilingual school just a few blocks due east of the ocean. Her parents admit that they first chose the school mostly out of convenience, when one of Jovanna's older sisters was attending another school around the corner from Colegio Inglés. In the crazy schedule they adhere to—over the border to work, back across to live—one trip for two girls made sense. But now that her sister has graduated Jovanna continues at the Colegio. Julia Venegas sees the advantages of this. The courses are taught mostly in English. Though José objects to the fact that the curriculum is nondenominational rather than Catholic, he acquiesces to his wife's desire to keep Jovanna enrolled. (Julia, born Catholic, is now Protestant, one of an increasingly large number of converts of Mexican origin). So the Venegas car takes the same route each day for the rest of the week, Wednesday to Miércoles, Friday to Viernes, and back again across the border. South to school in the madrugada, back across la frontera in the evening.

Light—luz, light—is light, though, isn't it? And the dark, oscura, sombra, it's the same in San Diego as it is in Tijuana. You find the same morning light in Playas—five blocks south of Border Field Park—pouring in through the windows where Jovanna stands at attention and prepares to participate in the opening morning exercises in the upper school and the same morning light in Imperial Beach, or along Route 75 along the Silver Strand, or up in La Jolla or over in Mission Hills. The same. Lo mismo. Igual. Evenings overtake you with the same oscuridad, yes? Sí!

Yes?

No!

American light plus Mexican light taken together equals more light than on either side of the border.

And Jovanna switches back and forth from English to Spanish so easily she holds that double light in her mind.

And a flawless accent in two languages.

Listen to her, look. It's convocation time, and two hundred kids from the upper school are celebrating the holidays of the month. She is marching up to the stage of the large shivery-cold school auditorium (no heat in these buildings in winter so in class all the students wear their coats and heavy sweaters), paper flowers draped across the front of her sweater. The students have lined up in neat rows, a color guard has marched in with the national flag and the flag of Baja California, one of the teachers flips a switch on a tape player, and the students launch into the strains of the Mexican national anthem. And then, much to the chagrin of a visiting pilgrim from New Jersey, they sing the nearly endless anthem of the state of Baja California. Chorus after chorus. (And standing there out of respect for the national colors, the pilgrim thinks to himself, What if all those years ago in the auditorium of the grammar school on Barracks Street in Perth Amboy, New

Jersey, after the salute to the flag and the singing of the national anthem he had had to memorize and sing, even once a week, the state song of New Jersey! And what would it have been? Anything like this long and melodic paean to the glories of Baja California? who knows, who knows? oh, New Jersey! oh, lost time!)

And then his cover is blown, somebody turns a flashlight on the fly on the wall!

Liz Hernández, head of the English program at the school, asks the students to greet the visiting writer from Washington, D.C. All heads turn toward the pilgrim, and he waves, feeling like the "sixty-year-old smiling public man" in Yeats's beautiful poem "Among School Children," arguably one of the greatest works of art ever written about knowledge and how we get it, and how we keep it, and how we see it, and the pilgrim, his head swimming with thoughts of Yeats and poetry, says, "Hi, kids," and tries to recover his cover. Why would she do that? he wonders. To keep the students on their best behavior, sure. But there's another reason, he figures. They are getting recognized! recognized for their work in English. Someone is paying attention to them, and though that makes kids nervous it also makes them walk taller, gives them a proper sense of importance. Because who, if not these kids, is important to the future of the city and the region? What if, what if, when he was a student at the grammar school some journalist/writer had come to watch him perform his morning exercise? What if in those days when he felt so small and ineffectual, when his dream world was so much larger than the actual world through which he moved (in a small circle through his small factory town on the Raritan River back in Jersey), someone had come to watch his progress and record his passage and to listen, with a keen ear cocked, for the music of his language? Why, then, he might have made music!

Look at Jovanna, for example. It's her turn to recite something appropriate for this almost Valentine's day celebration:

Roses are red,
Violets are blue,
Going to school,
Is super cool…

Her languid U.S. rhythms take the starch out of the more sharply defined accents of the other children who speak in English. Vowels and consonants bump up against each other like boxcars in a train wreck when some of the other children speak.

But then every student in the auditorium launches into the next song, and all's lovely again in accent-land. Stutterers can sing without a hitch, and children all around the world, not just here in Playas, sing American pop music with all of the liquidity of Mick Jagger imitating the Delta blues. So what do these kids sing? After the super-gooey nationalistic lyrics of the national and state anthems, they leap into an educational TV American-English pop hit.

Every day when you're walking down the street
And everybody that you meet
Has an original point of view
And I say hey!
[and the kids really hit it to accent the echoing]
HEY!
What a wonderful kind of day!
If we could learn to work and play
And get along with each other…

They're bobbing and weaving, they're bopping and snapping their fingers, to the theme song from *Arthur*, and

Hey!
What a wonderful kind of day!

when you can move your hands and feet and hips and shoulders to a sweet and lively little song like this and show off your English at the same time.

And

Hey!

It's so exhilarating when you can walk into a large space like this and hear all these kids putting out their voices and sounding something like native speakers.

2—*A Plan for Immersion*

Which was part of the vision of the founder of Colegio Inglés from the very beginning. Twenty-five years ago Evangelina Contreras de Elizondo and her sister Rita found themselves with school-age daughters and no school that they found satisfactory. So they started Colegio Inglés as a family business, with about eighty children in that first year. Their father, Dr. Contreras, is one of Mexico's leading holistic practitioners and his Oasis Hospital still stands a few blocks away from Colegio Inglés, across the street from the bull ring and literally almost a stone's throw from the border fence. Evangelina had a bilingual education in her elementary school in Mexico City, and she wanted the same for her own children.

"English is the lingua franca," Evangelina explains, "the language you need for business and travel and communications worldwide." So even if she hadn't been living just a few blocks from the border with the United States, she would have put forward the same educational plan. Opening first with a preschool program in the mid-seventies, she watched it grow with the city, adding on elementary classes and then the upper grades as the need arose from year to year. In 1987, her husband, Eliud Elizondo, joined her in the management of the expanding enterprise. Playas de Tijuana, before the road from the eastern part of the city opened in 1969, was a remote village. But once people could drive safely over the steep hill that separates it from the rest of the city, it expanded rather rapidly and now is home to over twenty thousand people, many of them middle-class professionals. What used to be just a weekend beach neighborhood became a real neighborhood, with its own council head and members, its own supermarkets and discount stores, its own Blockbuster Video—and a new Pentecostal Christian church, Iglesia de San Pablo, just around the corner from the Blockbuster.

It's not just an accident of geography that these two new buildings stand so close together. Not only has the infrastructure of Tijuana crept west over the big hill to Playas, but so has one of the most interesting phenomena in modern Mexican society, the growth of Pentecostal Christianity, Methodism, and Presbyterianism. By some estimates the number of Pentecostals in Mexico has gone from about 5 percent to nearly 20 percent since the end of World War II. (This has had an effect on the Mexican Catholic Church, producing, among other things, a charismatic Catholicism that tries to make traditional Catholicism more inviting to the young people who have been abandoning the Church for the Pentecostal sects.)

Playas has a high concentration of Pentecostals, thus the new church.

Evangelina and Eliud, for example, met at a Methodist church. And many of these people teach at Colegio Inglés—about half the teaching staff is Pentecostal rather than Catholic—and many send their children to Colegio Inglés, although the majority of the student population is Catholic.

The school has a good reputation, and also a reputation for its particular religious perspective. For some families it hasn't been easy to enroll their children there. Take the Venegas family, for example. José was born Catholic and remains Catholic. Julia was born Catholic but is now Pentecostal. They had a bit of a "discussion," as Julia puts it, when it came time to enroll Jovanna in Colegio Inglés. José wasn't so sure about it. He wanted a traditional education for his child. But he also wanted a good program of instruction in English and a location convenient to his older daughter's school. In this case, these latter points won out over tradition.

The school's growth suggests that a lot of people have been making similar decisions. Colegio Inglés now enrolls over five hundred students, from preschool on up through high school— the only grades missing are seventh and eighth, because Rita Contreras started her own school for those grades in another part of town, and the family tries to avoid competition, if it can. Like Mexico itself, the school is bottom-heavy with young students. (The high school program has in the last few years only just begun to get off the ground.)

When you walk into the patio of the lower school on Calle Pedregal, you can almost feel the potential of all of the students' power in the very walls and concrete of the place. You find yourself surrounded on three sides by several stories of classrooms, and you find names on the side of the walls: looking to the west, it's "Window to the Sky," and to the north, "Sing It to the Sea," the titles of particular courses of study in the series of textbooks chosen by Liz Hernández. For the past five years, Hernández has been the driving force behind the school's English language program. And over the course of his weeklong stay at the school, the pilgrim sees her as his guide in his progress up and down the staircases from floor to floor, from one classroom to the next, from one building to another, with a tour of Playas thrown in for good measure.

Hernández, now forty-seven and a career educator, talks as she and the pilgrim make these rounds. About her transborder family and her own life in education and in English education in particular.

She calls her family's history "a Mexican success story." Her father was born in the small central Mexican state of Aguascalientes and moved to San Diego at an early age where, among other things, he went to work selling newspapers at the train station—*next occupation?* Her mother grew up in Mazatlán and came to Tijuana to work as a seamstress. There she met the man from Aguascalientes and married him, and had three children, two boys, one now a physician and the other a computer expert, and Hernández, the teacher. She was the middle child, born in Mercy Hospital. In her early years she spoke mostly English at home with her father.

"Say it in English," he would tell her when she tried to speak with her mother in Spanish. She attended her first few years of school at San Ysidro Academy and crossed over to Tijuana for third grade knowing scarcely any Spanish at all.

It was at this early age that she discovered the uses of language immersion, picking up enough Spanish in a month to keep up with her schoolmates both as students and friends. (Yes, the pilgrim thinks to himself [in English, of course], immersion is the best way, as most linguistics experts will tell you, especially immersion at an early age since the child's mind soaks up language like a sponge and learns the rules of grammar and syntax intuitively. And immersion is historically the way that most people who have left a country and a language behind and come to America to make a new life have learned. Immersion has served as the baptism of American citizenship for most immigrant groups. Immersion is the heat atop which the American melting pot simmers and without it none of us would have mixed with the others in the ways that we need to in order to make a national culture. Greeks would have stayed more Greek than American and Italians more Italian than American and Yiddish speakers more Jewish than American and Serbs more Serbian than American. And who wants to live in a country that's as Balkanized as that, with little tribal wars raging through neighborhoods and cities over the primacy of one immigrant language over another? Imagine it, Chicago becoming something like a tribal crossroads, with language battles going on between the Poles and the Lithuanians and the Mexicans. Or like medieval Belgium, with its wars between the Flemish and the Walloons? Who wants that? Not this pilgrim, no, sir. Nyet, gospodin. No, señor. Non, madame. But then another part, the contentious part, of the pilgrim's mind leaps into the discussion, and suggests that what we see happening in California is a special case, and that Spanish needs to be given its due because, historically, it was one of the first languages of the region and of course because of the large numbers of residents who still speak it as a first language and of course because of the shared southern border with Spanish-speaking Mexico. Nyet, nyet! Why not then install Canadian English as a prime language in the United States because we share a northern border? Why not teach students in Vermont and

Minnesota and North Dakota and Montana to say "aboout" when they mean "about"? Ochi, ochi! Non, non! Nobody's making any judgments about the value of any of these other languages—though the English First movement might hold some who would argue, in that rationally developed insanity that seems to have infected some of the far right movements in post–Cold War America, that English is a better language than the others. This pilgrim laughs. He's quite sure that most of the people who hold to this view haven't read anything in English besides a translation of *Mein Kampf* and a comic book or two. No, this is practical. Nations need national languages because national cultures don't evolve without them. Just as Henry Higgins wants to instruct Eliza Doolittle in the language of Shakespeare, Milton, and the Bible, the pilgrim wants all Americans to have the opportunity to imbibe Hawthorne and Melville and Thoreau and Emily Dickinson in the original.)

However, none of this was in the air when the Hernández family moved to National City in 1967 just before Liz was ready for higher education. She attended Sweetwater High and then went on to study at Southwestern College for two years and then at San Diego State, certain that she would make a career in education herself. After college, she married a man who ran P.E. programs in the Tijuana public schools. In 1974, she answered an advertisement in the Tijuana newspaper and interviewed for a job at Colegio Inglés. She clicked at once with the Contreras sisters and went to work for them. But after the devaluation of the peso, she decided to take a job back across the border as a teacher at the now-defunct Clairemont Christian High School and then in 1988 as director of extended classes at Audubon Elementary in Spring Valley.

Twenty years after her first job at Colegio Inglés, she returned to Playas to take the job of English coordinator. While voters on the other side of the fence from Playas were about to go to the polls and take a stand against bilingual education, Hernández, recalling the success of her own immersion in Spanish when she first moved back to Tijuana and attended third grade, created an all-inclusive plan for immersing young Mexican students in English. Examining the possibilities, she chose a series of textbooks published by McGraw-Hill that put forward a so-called new view of English immersion. A multi-grade program, the texts emphasize the learning of English by means of poetry and music, especially by means of singing. While the teaching wars raged in the United States between the forces of phonics and the powers of "whole language," Liz Hernández chose to pick and choose among these two seemingly opposite approaches, using phonics when it seemed important, choosing the "whole language" approach at other times when common sense dictated.

"I use a 'learning style' that offers something for everybody," she says as we climb the stairs to the third floor of the lower building. It's still quite early in the school day and though the sun has risen good and strong above the hill above the Ensenada highway to the east, the halls remain chilly. And, as though the special effects man had just been salting the set with school odors, there's a medicinal smell wafting from the bathrooms, which for a moment takes the pilgrim back to his own school hallways in a place far away and rather long ago. And then he's listening to Liz Hernández and feeling the chill again on his face and hands. "The main thing is that we teach English as though it were a native tongue. We don't like the way bilingual programs are taught in the States. Even though I believe that sometimes confusion is necessary to instruction, bilingual instruction is confusing to the child in the worst ways. I know that because I taught in such programs in the States. And even though teachers are taught and trained to implement it, there's a problem built in to this plan of instruction. The teachers don't really expect as much from these students as they do from others. Most of the parents I worked with didn't like bilingual classes either. They would come to me and ask if we could please put their children in classes where only English was spoken. They didn't want their kids to be second-class students. Which is what happens to them by default in bilingual instruction."

A few children rush past in their haste to reach their classes on time.

"Good morning, Miz Liz," they say on the run.

"Good morning, children," Hernández says in a sweet and loving voice.

"Good morning, Mr. Cheuse," they toss over their shoulders as they move.

"Good morning, kids," the pilgrim says.

Hernández pauses, smiles at him. "In our program," she says, "children are taught to think in whatever language they're speaking. I keep going back to my own third-grade experience. That showed me the way. Immersion means no translating, everything is explained in context. Immersion makes for higher expectations from students." We reach our destination, a classroom on the third floor. "Here, you'll see." Hernández opens the door. The pilgrim dives in.

Third-grade math class, sixteen kids, boys in school sweaters and slacks, many wearing their coats because of the cold, girls in their jumpers, and they're wearing their coats, teacher in similar sweater and skirt, on the blackboard charts recording equivalences of inches and centimeters, the teacher quizzing on addition problems, all of this going on in English, including the under-conversation of the kids among themselves.

Imagine Liz Hernández about forty years ago, having crossed

over the border to attend school and thrown into this pool and learning to swim in the language.

But these kids haven't crossed over, not many of them. They were born in Tijuana and live in Tijuana, and they are learning math in English. A remarkable development, and with the exception of certain foreign language schools around the United States conducted for the children of foreign nationals—such as the Ecole Francaise in New York City—quite unusual.

The pilgrim picks up the math textbook, a multi-colored production, and flips through the pages, only to discover that some other kind of accounting is going on here besides math. As in all elementary textbooks, there are drawings and illustrations, but in this book they range from baseball—to a poem about Easter. Alongside a drawing of the Holy Spirit, the poem is laid out along the right-hand side of the page:

E is for the Eternal King
of whom we love to sing

A is for the God Almighty
who died for you and me

S is for the Spotless Lamb
the Holy Seed of Abraham

T is for the Timeless One
God's Everlasting Son

E is for the Earnest Saviour
who is our Open Door

R is for the Righteous King
of Whom we Love to Sing

The math class roars along, the kids helping, spurring each other on, while the teacher oversees them all like a coach with an athletic team. A few kids seem to take to math in a natural and easy way. Others stumble along, but all in English, with most of them caught up in the problems. What Easter has to do with any of this is hard to see.

Is there a Pentecostal mathematics? Well, if you look at the number of the Trinity, you might say yes, there is. It's a new number, trumping the decalog of the Old Testament. But no time to figure this out now. Time to change classes.

Moving across the hall into a third-grade English class, the pilgrim takes a closer look at the text, published by A Beka Book in Pensacola, Florida. His heart sings. On top of the wonderful spectacle he is beginning to see unfold before him, the hundreds of Mexican school children immersing themselves in the language that he loves and loves to write and read in, he stumbles on an important document, a prefatory essay to one of the textbooks that includes a treasure trove of things to think about in relation to American education. This document, titled "A Christian Approach to Reading," has to be, he considers as he reads it, the Constitution or the Magna Carta of Christian-oriented publishing in North America. He feels, to be sure, an initial shock, maybe just a volt or two, nothing that does more than set his hands tingling as he holds the book, at seeing the word "Christian" at the heart of this. The pilgrim is a product through and through, faults and good points (though mostly faults, he thinks) of public education. And he was raised a Jew, though now in midlife he finds himself a rather secular version of a dreamy mystic with practical leanings toward the practices, if not the wisdom, of the East. Nevertheless, the words of Laurel Hicks, the editorial director of A Beka Book, their ideas and their particular intelligence, begin to change right then and there the pilgrim's view of this particular variety of sectarian education.

The document opens with an epigram, an Emily Dickinson poem, yes, Emily Dickinson, except for her measured meters, not the sort of aesthetic experience that we know-it-alls about culture tend to expect Christian-oriented educators to read, let alone extoll.

> *He ate and drank the precious words,*
> *His spirit grew robust;*
> *He knew no more that he was poor,*
> *Nor that his frame was dust.*
> *He danced along the dingy days,*
> *And this bequest of wings*
> *Was but a book. What liberty*
> *A loosened spirit brings!*

It then begins: we have the opportunity to give our students wings—the wings of liberty that grow from the ability to read.

Nothing to argue with here, the pilgrim says to himself as he keeps going, while in the room along with him fifteen or so third-graders are making sentences that they will soon read aloud.

"Many modern educators believe that reading is not an important skill for all children to learn. We are moving away from the age of print, they say, and into the age of the machine. With the advent of the radio, television, and other devices, reading is no longer the only way to obtain necessary information. Those who cannot read well, we are told, can learn from others—

others can tell them what to do, what to think, and what to believe..."

Yes, the pilgrim thinks, this Christian educator is on to something here, the way she couches the glib arguments of the new Philistines who walk hand in hand into the new Millennium with the new Totalitarians. The bland leading the not so bland. It's something that sends shivers up the spine of writers and poets, this vision of a world in which "other devices," i.e., the computer, will guide the not so well educated toward the heaven of the sound-bite and the headline, the mini-quotation and the sleepwalking life that used to know style and context rather than excerpt and simple sentences only. (Consider the maligning of the style of old Hemingway, whose complexities lie beneath the seemingly simple surfaces, like some croc lurking beneath still waters in the bright light of day—but that's another story. Not now, when the kids all around are trying to make simple sentences in a language not their own and the pilgrim is reading this manifesto on something he thought before he began to read it that he would disagree with ever so strongly.)

"If our country is to remain a land of liberty," Ms. Hicks continues, "we must continue to teach each individual to read and think on his own. We cannot afford to allow even our slowest students to develop the attitude that others can do their thinking for them...Reading is necessary to democracy. It is necessary for those who would expand the horizons of their own small worlds..."

An important argument, a bold argument. Yes, because who can imagine our form of government and a population that cannot read, or at least not read beyond the level of the simple sentence? The two don't mix. We began as a Republic because the majority of the population didn't read. We matured as a democracy because the majority of the population could read. And on what verge do we now stand looking across the abyss of the Y2K myth toward the new Millennium? The advent of the call to erase this new so-called computer illiteracy can make a writing and reading person's knees quake if you see computer literacy leading to a radical new illiteracy of mind and heart.

So despite the pilgrim's initial biased response to the title of this little essay, he now saw himself allied with this Beka Book editor in defense of reading, the rope ladder that the gods had lowered down to him in the pit where he lived as a child in central New Jersey, so that he might catch hold of it and climb out into the world and the light. Yes, reading was a weapon in the war against totalitarian mind-catching, and it was also a home for the mind, a place in which to dwell, a vessel from which to drink and also to travel in, from country to country and world to world of the mind of others, other times, other places. To live and not to read was to inhale and not to breathe, to walk and not to move, to eat and not to taste, to kiss and not to love. Reading isn't just necessary for democracy, it's a necessity for consciousness. It is the single most important invention of our species after fire, and without it we live only a glorified version of the life of brutes in caves. Storytelling is for children, and that's why we regard the age of the Homeric epic as the childhood of our civilization. Reading announces our maturity. If we stop, we will know that we will soon be dead as individual minds and as a culture.

And then came the next sentence in this little pamphlet in the war against ignorance. "It is especially necessary for Christians, because God has given us a written revelation—the Bible—and we need to be able to read it accurately and with understanding..." So there it was, out in the open, the theological imperative to read.

An interesting twist. Reading is good because it allows you to read the Word of God, which He wrote down in the Bible for all to see.

The pilgrim felt a little shudder right then and there in that classroom, perhaps because of the lack of heat in the school, perhaps because he understood the argument and found himself not entirely unaligned with it. Wasn't his own tribe known as the People of the Book because of its historical and theological ties to the Old Testament?

And yet he understood the argument to be reactionary and retrograde. To believe reading was valuable because it came from God? He was much too modern and much too secular to believe that he ought to believe this.

And yet everything that he understood to be true (whatever that word meant) about his great love, the epics of the Homeric period in the pre-classical Mediterranean, suggested that these poems might have come from the gods. The poets believed that they did. They cocked their ears toward the heavens and Mnemosyne, the goddess after whom centuries later the function of memorizing would be named, said the words of the poems to them in order that they might repeat them to the audience. The poets were mere conduits for the words of the goddess. Or else they memorized and gave the credit to the goddess. That's the practical, secular way to think about it. But since what we call, as the later Greeks did, memory is the translation of the name of the goddess Mnymosyne, it's possible to imagine that first came the goddess and later came the imitation of the process that she instructed poets to use.

So if he believed that this might be possible, if not the actual truth, then why couldn't he consider it possible that the God of the Old Testament and New gave the words of the biblical text to his followers?

Too many textual problems, that's why. And did God choose to include the Gospel of John and not the Gospel of Timothy? Yes, too many apocryphal manuscripts as well as those riddled with textual problems.

But—and the pilgrim is still daydreaming over this document while the kids in the room are copying some of their sentences on the blackboard—you could say that God inspired the authors of the Biblical texts and if they made errors in transcribing, or in the editing of the various versions of the texts, that error is human. The delivery is divine.

The rest of the document is quite fascinating, but the pilgrim has to skim through it quickly. Hicks goes on to argue that the phonics approach is the best, but by fifth grade the good readers shouldn't need it anymore. And that historically American textbooks from the New England Primers on through McGuffey and Swinton and Cyr recognized that school children needed instruction in Christian principles, a tradition in which A Beka Book is following. All the rest of the books teachers choose for their students, Hicks suggests, should come out of "the vast storehouse of the best literature of the ages"—and when the pilgrim reads that, his heart glows. Yes, the best. Homer, Virgil, Chaucer, Dante, Shakespeare, Cervantes. But then Hicks goes on to say that the books the teachers choose should have "character-building themes" that are developed through in a natural 'non-preachy' way..." Ok. Homer, Virgil, Chaucer, Dante, Cervantes, Shakespeare...But Hicks then concludes by urging educators to "choose books that are true to Biblical principles. Where do you find books such as these? she asks. At A Beka Book, a place not lately lauded for its editions of Homer, Virgil, Chaucer, Dante, Shakespeare, and Cervantes."

3—Creation Acceleration

The pilgrim feels a bit confused. But he doesn't have time to mull this over right now, and instead looks to the blackboard to see a few sentences that some students are copying there, which are then corrected by the instructor, all of this back and forth done in English.

> *To build a snowman you have to make the balls big. Then the gloobs.* [gloves, the instructor corrects]

> *The snowman is with snow. With a carrot. With stcs.* [sticks]
> *And racs.* [rocks?]

And then, whoops, the bell rings, class is over, the pilgrim has been daydreaming about the material on Christian readers, daydreaming just as he did almost all the way through his own school years.

(—oh, no, you can't go into a school after a certain age and not think back to your own education, or is there another name for it, what happened to you when you were young and in classrooms?—and once again the smell of the hallways takes the pilgrim back—and won't immediately release him—back to his hometown in New Jersey, with its umbrella of smoke from the oil refineries and the small factories that surrounded it, and the slender, rocky beach and splintering old boardwalk and piers smelling of tar on the southern edge along the half-mile-wide river, the salvationary river that flowed into the bay where foreign tankers lay at anchor and a small lighthouse marked the boundary between these waters and the ocean called Atlantic. Fifty years ago the pilgrim tried to make sentences in his own third-grade class and fifty years ago he scoured the beach for lucky stones to skip out over the gentle lapping surf and dug for small crabs that he stored in jars so that he could watch them wriggle and

writhe and after a time he released them into the surf where the
water sank into the sand and now and then a dead horseshoe
crab washed up, stinking of iodine and rotting meat, and fifty
years ago he sat in a room with others his age and added and
subtracted and divided, never noticing the years passing by, never
counting the years that lay ahead, and English sounded to him like
a foreign language when his immigrant father spoke it, and when
his immigrant great-grandmother spoke it and when his maternal
grandfather spoke it, even though he was unaware that he was
speaking a language particular to a particular place and nation and
culture, no, at that age, and younger, you speak a language that
you take to be the language of life itself, language that comes to
you as naturally when you open your mouth to speak as air does
when you take a breath…)

"You're going to see the Delta students now," Liz Hernández
says, pointing the pilgrim to another classroom door. "Delta is the
all-English program for accelerated students."

And accelerate they do, inscribing sentences on the blackboard
one after another—

> *The sun is hot. The sun is yellow. The*
> *sun is in the sky—*

with the alacrity of native speakers of English their own age (and
the pilgrim watching them, sees them move their hands in the
cursive manner, the curves and twists of letters looping and lines
crossing back seems almost to describe the passage of a mind
surging toward the light, because education at its best is never a
straight march forward but rather a loop-de-loop amusement park
ride, yes, it's exhilarating, it's dangerous, it makes the blood rush
and strain at the inner walls of the arteries, it upsets the brain,

and if when you're studying you feel none of this then something
is very wrong and not with you but with your instructors, oh,
and the pilgrim remembers his own rote learning days, when
making sentences consisted of diagramming sentences, the noun
and the verb on one line, the modifiers and other parts of speech
pointing away up or down from the main progress, and this was
supposed to be a science but it taught only confusion, because
the only way you can really learn how to make a good sentence
is to read good sentences and in the United States the good
modern sentence was created in the laboratories of sorcerers
Gertrude Stein and Sherwood Anderson and followed up by
the work of their apprentice Ernest Hemingway—their young
hands hovering like birds above the letters, the words, the
sentences, as his own daughters and son did years ago, in the moist
years of their early school days, as his own hands moved even
many more years ago in the shadowy rooms of the dilapidated
nineteenth-century buildings that housed the elementary classes
he attended in that same Jersey factory town, the hands moving
like those of a sorcerer, motioning for a letter to appear here,
a letter there, next to it, and soon the word, and then another
word, and then a sentence ["The sun is hot. The sun is yellow.
The sun is in the sky..."]—

Oh, Christian reader, Catholic and Hebraic readers, oh,
Muslim, oh, Hindu, and all of you followers of whatever
other religions on earth, was it not this way at the moment of
creation? when God or the Gods or the gods made something
out of nothing, the stuff of us, the original star dust that is our
ancestral matter, when they writ large the word cosmos and
the galaxies appeared outlined against the dark matter, first
things begin as lines melding into curves and making letters
making words, a noun, and then a verb, even the to-be verb

connoting nothing but essential existence, And there was light. Before that, darkness upon the face of the waters, not even the waters, only the words of Deity, and there was light, the spoken sentence about light of which for true believers the sentence on the page is the mere shadow of the act, for the world is a book, was once the way the great Western theologians regarded the realm they inhabited, and one had to learn to interpret it the way one interpreted a text on papyrus or, later, between covers, bound and laying flat upon a desk, all the universe contained with the covers, and this was a time when reading and knowing God were one and the same, and then reading was seized by the bishops as a right, and Luther stood against the sole interpreters of the Biblical scripture, and then reading became a privilege of the rich and titled classes, and then of the landed gentry and their wives, and then trickled down to their children's tutors and their housemaids and then became, like weather, endemic in the West, so that in our age illiteracy, once the norm, is now considered a problem and an embarrassment and those who cannot read inhabit an alternative universe to our own, living on their instincts and the kindness of those who can read—Hebrew proverb, When someone dies, a universe is lost—emend to When a reader is born, a universe lights up—["The sun is hot. The sun is yellow. The sun is in the sky..."]—

Admit it, watching these children make their sentences is like observing moving versions of the photographs from the Hubble telescope, seeing galaxies born, like being witness to the beginning of civilization as wild egos learn the rules of spelling and the wily turns and necessities of syntax, the essence of the organization of chaos!

The pilgrim sees it in the fifth-grade grammar and reading class he goes to now, where twenty-five students work so hard at making sentences they seem to raise the temperature in the cold room—little factories of knowledges, they plunge into the construction of language, each of them a God making a world out of the noises we make with our tongues and lips and throats. The teacher asks about their reading projects.

An eleven-year-old boy named Jorge announces that he's reading Jules Verne's *Twenty Thousand Leagues Under the Sea*. The pilgrim nods, approves (thinking to himself, that's a lot better reading than he did when he was that age, having only "read" that particular novel in one of the old *Classics Illustrated* comic-book editions, which was the first time he encountered a number of great works of art from the Homeric epics on through Poe— maybe, he thinks, that his "visual" period, all the comic books he read and collected when he was that age is the equivalent of the oral period in Western culture, when the Homeric poets recited their tens of thousands of lines of verse that had been delivered to them by Mnymosyne, yes, and so he could say that he went from the visual to the literal, though the comic books always did have some words, Homer's or Jules Verne's or Poe's or George Eliot's in those little speech balloons that hovered over the heads of the figures in the drawings, and if he could have as an adult without prior experience of reading comics, an adult, say, with a classical education, seen himself at that age, surrounded by tons of comic books, the classical stories and *Archie* and horror comics such as *The Heap* and *The Hulk* or *EC Horror Stories*, he probably would have concluded that he was observing a lost boy, a pre-literature turd-head who, like most people in New Jersey wouldn't know a caesura from a Roman emperor—but there is hope for a lost boy in Jersey, isn't there, when he can go from comics to classic comics to classics? It takes time, but he can make the climb, it takes only a love of literature, of story, of the wide-ranging imagination that builds worlds, and where did it begin for him, he wonders even now as other children in this classroom in Playas stand and announce the titles of the books they're reading—a number of bland and unfamiliar names to his ears, maybe these are the good Christian books advocated in the Beka Book manifesto, good, and thus boring—but where did it begin for the pilgrim? starting at rest? in the bedtime stories his father read him in Russian from a musty old sepia-colored book that smelled of wood and oranges? and then on to comic books? and to the *Classics Illustrated*? because after that came adventure novels about the sea, and science-fiction stories and novels, and many after-school and weekend visits to the musty old hometown library—you entered through the main doors and then turned sharply to the right and took the long tunnel to the children's library to the rear of the main building, but before too long the young pilgrim would stop at the display of new books at the adult entrance and there he found intriguing titles such as *Invisible Man* and *The Castle* and *The Mystery of Edwin Drood*, books he flirted with every time he walked past the special display shelf, and as the days went by, he must have been above eleven now, he would stop and pluck one of these from the shelf and study its cover and turn its pages, yes, even sniff them, entranced by the special and peculiar and annealing odor of good book paper, the kind of paper you only find today in special editions—do you remember holding a book up to your nose and inhaling the scent of it? as though the narrative itself were a magic powder to be inhaled so that it went straight to the brain?—and as the months went by he picked up one of these books and read a little, it was, he clearly recalls, Ellison's *Invisible Man*, and every time he took up the book he would get a little further but then return it to the shelf, each time a little less confused by the language but still in a quandary about it and unable to track the story, until an autumn a few years later when he kept the book out and went to the children's section and flopped onto a big leather sofa and read it all the way through, and who knows, as Ellison's nameless narrator says at the end of that novel, but on the lower frequencies the pilgrim's experience speaks for yours?—and after the reading began for him, then came the writing, and though he knows that the latter always grows out of the former, he does remember Sundays when he was a child listening to his father clacking away at an old typewriter in an alcove off the living room in the apartment his family inhabited a half block or so from the river, clackety-clacking away on stories in English, his father's second language, about life in the Old Country, and that picture of his father hunched over the typewriter trying to write stories must have burned into his mind, an emblem of a life he thought must be a good one because the man he admired so much at that time his father was living it, so, yes, though he knows that reading makes writing he also understands that living makes writing, or perhaps you need both of these, the living and the reading to come together in a particular way and lo, you have an artist, that creature over whose soul the Gods worry more than most other living creatures because they need the help more than most!

The reading never far from the writing, the writing never far from reading and life, there is a description, if not a prescription for how one makes one's way in this world of noise and sights and tastes and fears and loves.)

["The sun is hot. The sun is yellow. The sun is in the sky."]

The pilgrim surfaces from the deep pool of his recollections to discover that it is Jovanna Venegas's turn to talk about her reading project.

"What is the name of your book?" the teacher says.

"*The Cobra Project*," says Jovanna.

The pilgrim can't believe what he's hearing. He couldn't be more shocked and surprised if she had announced that she was reading one of his own novels. Here is this eleven-year-old, reading a popular U.S. novel of a few years back by a gifted nonfiction writer—Richard Preston—turned novelist, on the subject of the possibility of biological terrorism in the United States, a novel that the pilgrim himself had devoured when it first appeared and, because it was so good, passed around, as he sometimes did with entertaining books, to members of his family. An eleven-year-old with his own taste in popular fiction! (which calls the pilgrim back to another schoolroom, one he visited only this past autumn, in Miami, where, after a talk he gave about the life of the writer to a group of seventy or eighty high school juniors and seniors, one of the nastiest, baldest, baddest-looking dudes in the audience came sauntering up to him and asked him if he could ask him a personal question and when the answer was yes, asked if the pilgrim knew about a book he happened to be reading, it was called *The Critique of Pure Reason* by Emmanuel Kant. Well, yes, once he had studied Kant, the pilgrim said, not adding that it was so long ago that he had only two reactions, astonishment at the young fellow's choice of reading and dismay at his own distance from such an important philosophical tract of which he recalled nothing at all.)

So here's this fifth grader reading at his level. Is this just an accident or oddity or does it have something to do with the immersion program here at Colegio Inglés? Well, it's Jovanna and she lives on the other side of the border. She'd do well in any school. She'd be reading this novel anyway. Perhaps. But here she is, and this is where we are. And she's flourishing, immersed.

On to another class, Ms. Zulema Gracia's sixth-grade English course.

"Good morning, Mr. Cheuse," the school children say.

"Good morning, kids," the pilgrim once again responds.

omen

responsibility

jinx

guilt

In the front of the room, Ms. Zulema is writing the words of the day on the blackboard.

"What is an omen?" she asks of the group and a girl a fifth of the pilgrim's age gives a better answer than he could have back then and just as good as he could right now.

"And a jinx?" the teacher says.

Dark words, why these dark words? Why not cheerful happy ebullient Christian words? Well, yes, of course, there is a Pentecostal vocabulary. But omen? jinx? These are pagan words. Guilt and responsibility, yes, Christian, perhaps. Modern words, anyway. So the vocabulary is a mix. What about grammar? Is there such a thing as Pentecostal syntax? Or should we call it sin-tax? Or are we all in this together, noun and verb, modifiers abounding, musical phrases deep and high, light and dark?

"I understood the omen and saw that it was my responsibility; the guilt was mine; I was the jinx."

My sentence, not one of the children's. But they did almost as well.

"An omen tells you to feel guilt," a girl says.

"Don't jinx the omen," says a boy from the other side of the room.

"Guilt is my responsibility," says another student.

They're clustered together in two groups, one fifth grade, one sixth, the lower graders working on more sentences while the uppers get talked to by Ms. Zulema about the homework for the next session. Now and then one of the students glances the pilgrim's way. A lingering fog of self-consciousness in the room. But not much. The kids keep their heads bent over their work. Except for one boy in a group at the back of the room, there's no one even fidgeting. And Ms. Zulema has her eye on him, steadies him now and then with a word or two. How much more is an instructor at this level—she's part philosopher and part mother, part cowherd, sheepdog, jungle guide, goddess and goalkeeper.

On through the streams of students in the halls and stairwells to Ms. Rocio's class in another part of the lower school building. Her mother and sister also work here as teachers, and she and her sister were students at Colegio Inglés. As the pilgrim enters, the room quiets down. The students have just begun work, reading aloud a classical Chinese poem (in English translation) on friendship and love and discussing the meaning of the word "oath" that stands at the center of the poem. Ms. Rocio then asks them to write a poem on friendship. Heads bow, pencils move. After a while sharp girls read their poems. Shy boys keep their chins up as they recite their own work.

Later, in the hall, Liz Hernández leans toward the pilgrim and says, "Doesn't seeing these children in action give you hope?" before they move along to Mr. Dan's class. The morning is growing older. The school is a bit warmer now, with the sun having risen high above the hills on the other side of the Ensenada highway just to the east of the school grounds. Here's Mr. Dan: dark-haired, of medium height, a dapper Dan in his green school sweater and neatly pressed slacks, this instructor is part entertainer, cheerleader, magician, and song leader as he points out to his fourth graders some of the significant consonant combinations in the odd language we're all speaking. Consonants, vowels, sentences flutter in the air. The energy in the room is almost palpable. This teacher really pushes. And the kids rush ahead. And then, suddenly, rehearsal time. There's a big school fiesta coming up at the end of the week, when parents will come to see their kids perform. The music comes up, the class belts out a snappy rendition of "Arthur's Theme Song,"

And I say hey!
(HEY!)
What a wonderful kind of day
If we could learn to work and play
And get along with each other...

4—Recess

Whee! hey! the pace picks up as the bell rings announcing recess and kids in their sweaters and jumpers and polished tie shoes rush out of the halls into the patio. (How the pilgrim used to love recess! A break in the unrelenting time of the classroom, a rift in the wall, a tear in the fabric, so we could race around the stones of the school yard and throw our fists at each other and throw ourselves against the brick wall of the school and toss books into the air and toss balls and marbles and baseball cards and steal the shoes off the feet of the weaker boys and chase the girls and pull their hair and kiss the sun and shout into the rising morning—HEY!)

These kids do the same, in Spanish, yes, while out here in the yard it's mostly Spanish they nip and spit at each other, and hurl over each other's heads, and rush against in the push of the warming sun. Though now and then some of the students whose classes the pilgrim has visited veer off from the main flock of passing student cliques and slow down and come shyly forward toward the side of the patio to say hello.

"...Mr. Cheuse..."

"And how are you?"

"I'm fine."

"I'm glad to hear that. I enjoyed visiting your class."

A giggle. Three girls huddled together, giggling.

"Thank you. Thank you. Thank you."

Two handsome nine-year-old boys stagger over, twins, and the girls giggle their way away into the center of the yard again.

"Good morning," they say, almost in unison, and then rush away into the whirl of the yard.

Next comes a fifth-grade girl who speaks no English, an unroasted kernel in an otherwise smooth cereal mix. She and the pilgrim briefly converse, and then her friends swing by, giggling, of course, and offer him nacho chips and cola, not his style for snack or lunch and so he tries gracefully in his fifth-grade Spanish to decline the offer. The girls scurry off.

A teacher comes over, and she and the pilgrim sit and talk quietly in the sun. It's Ivy Flores, tall, with a reddish permanent, born in Mexico City. She studied English in school and spent her sophomore year in high school in Austin and attended the Autonomous University of Baja, in Ensenada. Her two sons attend Colegio Inglés, as do many other of the children of staff members. In front of her classroom, she was firm and yet welcoming. In the sun, she's a little shy when it comes to questions about her life.

There's Mr. Dan, hurrying past, working the recess hour. He holds two jobs, like many teachers, hit hard by the latest devaluation of the peso.

Here's Zulema Fernández Gracia, from Mexico City, twenty-five years old, short dark hair, graceful movements. Her father is a retired military officer who studied at a U.S. military academy, her mother a translator, which meant that her household was one where English was spoken fluently, something to which her own fluid near-accentless English attests. Her family moved to Tijuana when she was a young girl and this is where she met her husband, a graphic designer with whom she runs a small business. Ms. Zulema, as the students call her, is the mother of one small child and just this week has learned that she is pregnant again. This suggests a certain optimism to the pilgrim and he is not surprised by her thoughts about the future of her country.

"I think we're moving rapidly toward a serious multiple party system, and that's good," she says. "So I'm optimistic about Mexico. The future is ours. We have everything going for us, except that we seem always to be in a perpetual crisis. I have faith. Not in Zedillo. But in the ones who will come after him. Meanwhile we just have to keep our families strong and protect our children."

The children, the children! There's a different emphasis on protecting the children here in Mexico, compared to the United States. You sometimes hear parents in the United States talking about their kids and education, but never with this intensity about the kids themselves. It always sounds as though the parents want to protect the children's souls or the children's futures or the children's privileges (this last a hidden theme, but one that's present nonetheless if you scratch beneath the surface). Or else you hear parents talking about protecting their children against pornography or drugs or violence, or all three. Or you hear fundamentalist parents talking about protecting their children against the relativism of modern society. But what is it they are protecting, the pilgrim always wonders when he hears such talk. Do they know their children? Or are they protecting an idea of their children, not the kids themselves? He thinks about these things a lot, because having fathered three children and divorced two mothers, he has always striven to stay as good a father to his kids as he possibly could be, faltering here and there, out of ignorance, perhaps, but never out of lack of love or, worse, indifference. Yes, he has made his mistakes, but he has tried to learn from them. But nothing like attending elementary school again to make you think of your own past with your own children, and wondering how, if you had somehow kept the marriages together, how much better their lives might have been. His daughters, his son—how much do they hold against him for this? Well, maybe not the girls as much as the boy, because he was the firstborn, and while the firstborn gains more freedom more quickly, he also suffers for his freedom when the other children arrive, because he is no longer the only one in line. But how to protect these slender plants while they take on nourishment, these cubs in the den, how to keep them safe, and help them to become more of themselves, before it's their turn to wander out into the wilderness on their own? A question in rime comes to the pilgrim's mind, from W. B. Yeats's beautiful poem about life and death and education, "What youthful mother, a shape upon her lap / Honey of generation had betrayed, / And that must sleep, shriek, struggle to escape / As recollection or the drug decide, / Would think her son, did she but see that shape / With sixty or more winters on its head, / A compensation for the pang of his birth, / Or the uncertainty of his setting forth?"

None of these questions anything the pilgrim can fully answer quickly, especially not sitting here in the sun in the school patio at recess time, watching lean, wiry Rafael Enríquez coming toward him.

Rafe, or "Mr. Ralph" as he is known to the students, at nineteen is by far the youngest teacher on the staff. So even with his close-cropped brown hair and almost comical ears, he, unlike many nineteen-year-olds, can look in the mirror and see someone who has already accomplished something with his life. Like many inhabitants of this border region, he has a mixed and interesting background. Born in Orange County to a woman from Tijuana and an L.A. mechanic, he lived in Norwalk but moved south across the border to board with his grandmother and several uncles. He took his early grades at Colegio Inglés but then attended public high school in Tijuana. So he speaks with some expertise on the differences between public and private schools.

"At Colegio Inglés," he says, "students learn how to get along with other students. They learn manners and how to conduct themselves in a civil way. Public school is another world. Here it's safe, there it's a dangerous world." He's munching on chile flavored chips as he talks, a way of catching lunch on the fly. "I had such good teachers in my early years. 'Sit down and pay attention,' they'd tell me. 'Maybe you'll learn something new today.' They helped me to become confident in many different ways. When I had to sing, the teacher made me stand on top of the table to do it. I remember how much that helped me, so I know that if I become a good teacher I can make a difference in the lives of these kids. You have to start with the seed, to make good fruit."

Rafe is teaching first, third, and fourth grades at the Colegio Inglés and studying education at the Colegio Normal Enseñada. He hopes eventually, he explains, to teach in a public school, "where the kids need more attention." Meanwhile, he's got plenty of good stories about his work right now.

Almost with a blush, he says, "I like to work with the difficult ones, the ones who make trouble. Because I understand them. I could be like that." And he tells a story about how he engaged the trust of a fourth-grade boy, the worst bully in the class, a boy estranged from his father who asked Rafe if he could be his friend. Sure, Rafe, said, until one day during recess when he and the boy were talking and the boy suddenly excused himself, because he saw another student he wanted to beat up.

"'What do you mean?' I said to him. 'You can't just go up to that boy and beat him.' 'But I don't like him,' my little friend said. And I said, 'No friend of mine goes around beating on people.' He stopped, he looked at me, and he stayed where he was. I had done something. That's the kind of thing I want to do. One by one, you teach them these things. It makes me so happy to help a boy like that. It makes me feel joy inside."

A band of boys wheel past the stone wall where Rafe and the pilgrim sit, a scream of hawks with corresponding shrieks from the hawk-ettes in the middle of the patio. You can't say that these kids, coming up for air after their morning's English immersion, don't have a good time. Yes? the pilgrim looks to Rafe.

"Joy like that?"

"Yes," he says. "Joy like that."

Extraordinary, the pilgrim thinks to himself. A kid like this, nineteen years old, having been shuffled off by his parents to live with his grandmother and uncles—"They are like my brothers," he explained earlier—keeping pet chickens in the small house in a poor district of Tijuana, and not many years ago running around this same school yard in his green sweater and dark shoes, his head full of questions, his heart full with the pleasure of living in the world, no matter what his circumstances. Rafe, at nineteen, may be the greatest optimist and humanitarian the pilgrim has met in many years. And he has, like all of the staff here the pilgrim has spoken with, great hope for the future of his country which, as the sun creeps along toward signaling the end of recess and the beginning of the next round of classes, he expounds upon.

"I believe in the town, and I think of Mexico as a town, a big town, but still a town, and if everyone does his little job in his little place, all of that together will make the big things happen. Small things make the big things happen. Especially when we educate more and more of the people. With an educated population, we'll all do good things."

A light brighter than the sun on his face sparks into his eyes. He smiles. Nineteen. A new teacher. Raised by grandma. Keeps pet chickens. His uncles are his best friends. And some of his students. In his heart, great joy at doing what he does. And at the thought of doing what he hopes to do, even greater. And his smile stretches his cheeks almost to his ears. And tears well up in his eyes, and he weeps.

Ah, Mexico, what Yankee teacher would allow himself to show these dreams and emotions in the open in this way? No one the pilgrim has ever heard of. So perhaps there is hope. And perhaps there will be even greater joy.

The school bell clangs. End of recess. Rafe excuses himself and returns to his classroom, followed, like some mother duck or goose, by a gaggle of kids in sweaters and jumpers. Perhaps, if they pay attention, they'll learn something new today.

5—A Wonderful Kind of Day

Still early this Friday morning in Playas, though the sun has already daubed the clouds over the ocean with a dahlia-pink hue and illuminated the peaks of Las Coronadas, those small rocky islands due west of Tijuana, the last bit of Mexican territory to be touched by the light of day and the last to catch the light before night fully settles over the west. Even before the first of the children have arrived for class, in the chill air two workmen are unloading folding chairs from a small truck and lining them up against the far wall of the patio at the center of the Colegio Inglés lower school.

Up in Liz Hernández's office, a group of teachers are putting the finishing touches on cardboard signs. Ms. Zulema's there, cutting and pasting. She's making hearts. She's cutting out red and green paper to trim big signs. So is Ms. Rocio and Ms. Ivy. Mr. Dan pops in for a few minutes to help and departs. Rafe comes in carrying a bunch of paper headdresses with paper feathers, sets them down and works awhile on the signs, then picks up his headdresses and departs. Friends are Wonderful. We Love Friends. The signs announce the theme of the school's annual Friendship Day program, which will commence after the noon hour.

In the patio, small groups of students soon gather before class and rehearse bits and pieces of songs. Long lines of students pass up and down the stairs, more and more of them as the morning moves along, some of them already wearing pieces of costumes for the program they'll later perform. These otherwise usually well-behaved children can't seem to help but chatter away to each other, in Spanish and English. The sun is rising higher in the sky and the hour is getting closer and closer.

Oh, it's difficult to sit still in class today, with the program almost about to begin. The pilgrim wanders in and out of rooms, witness to such distraction as he recalls quite vividly from events of only fifty or more years before. The excitement of demonstrating your newfound skill to your mother and father. The giddiness that comes with having them become witness to your work and to make the acquaintance of your teachers. If any pride is pure, it is that sort of pride, the child revelatory before the inquisitive—and admiring—parent. And it goes on and on in life, doesn't it? with each accomplishment in school adding to the list of things you want to show to them. This is the sort of pride that, if it comes before a fall, comes before the loss of our parents and intimations of mortality. And for those with faith, the lucky ones as the pilgrim sometimes sees them, more often again than not, the lucky, yes, though they may lose their immediate parents they always have God before whom they can demonstrate, children always, wanting to please. But then what are we all anyway, with faith or without, if not still children wanting to please.

Woe, and if any parent fails to show interest! what a blow to the child's ego! what a quick way to poison the purity of the innocent child's desire! Because then, as the pilgrim well knows from his own childhood, the kid becomes a showoff and a noisemaker and a troublemaker, doing everything from spitting gum and flying paper airplanes to setting off firecrackers and stealing in order to get attention from the older generation. This is the zygote of the artist/outlaw, before the egg has begun to divide, the crossroads of a life that will be dedicated either to art or to its dark alternative, a life of crime. For how else does the disturbed child—and have no doubt about it, the artist almost from the start is as disturbed a character as the criminal—command the spotlight upon himself?

But these are questions for a more advanced exam than any that will be given in this school, or in most others, at least at this level, and the pilgrim puts them away in his school pack to deal with on another day. It's getting close to fiesta time, and he wanders back out onto the patio to watch the final preparations. A large folding screen now stands in mid-patio bedecked with all of those friendship signs that the teachers were working on earlier. Mr.

Dan is wrapping streamers around the pillars in the patio. One of the teachers is testing the loudspeaker system. Ms. Rocio is testing some tapes. A burst of music.

> *And I say hey!*
> *HEY!*
> *What a wonderful kind of day...*

Several grades worth of children are now lining up in various parts of the patio, rehearsing with their teachers, but the wind has picked up a bit and it's difficult to hear their songs over the noise of the loudspeaker. Another teacher sets up a microphone just in front of the folding screen and three boys drift over to her, scripts in hand, ready to rehearse their parts in the ceremonies.

When they come drifting past him, the pilgrim hails them from the cement bench where he has taken up residence to watch the events of the rest of the morning.

They are Alex and Luis and Carlos, nine years old, buddies in their early pre-adolescent coolness.

"How are you doing?" the pilgrim says.

"Good," says Alex, nodding to his friends. They nod back, and the three of them sit down next to him.

A conversation ensues, about school, about the show that's almost about to begin, about the quality of their English, which is first-rate.

"Oh, yeah," Alex says with a laugh. "We're the only ones in the school who can really speak English. That's why we'll be in front."

"Is that right?" the pilgrim says.

"Absolutely," says Luis.

"Uh-huh," Carlos puts in.

And what do they think of this school?

"It's okay," Alex says.

"Could be worse," Luis says.

"The high school is worse," Carlos says.

"Yeah, we hear about the high school," Alex says. "They're really strict, too strict. I don't want to go here to high school."

"Where to then?" the pilgrim says.

"Maybe in San Diego," Alex says.

"Sure," Carlos says.

"I'd like that, too," Luis says.

A teacher calls them over the loudspeaker.

"We have to go and talk English now," Alex says. "I told you, we're the only ones who can."

Their joking aside, these boys, along with girls like Jovanna Venegas, are certainly among the elite of the school's Anglophones, and in each of their cases helped along by the fact—the pilgrim continues to pursue a little questioning here at the bench in the sun—that at home there is either a parent or two or a sibling who speaks English with them. (Over in the upper school building, he knows from having snooped around there a bit after that first morning convocation, there are classes for parents who wish to learn English in order to help their kids along, and the oldest students in the school, those few at the high school level which is, paradoxically, the most recent level to be added to the curriculum, just seem to be stumbling along in a course in English as a second language. Because over the decades there has been no continuity at Colegio Inglés between the elementary and the junior high levels, the best students, those with a fluency in English that rivals that of the best U.S. students at the same grade level, go on to study at other schools both in Tijuana and San Diego.)

The pilgrim leans back on the bench as his fluent companions run off, enjoying the sun ["The sun is hot. The sun is yellow. The sun is in the sky."] and basking in the humor of their put-on. And remembering again the wiseass humor of his own student days—the notes passed, the paper airplanes launched, the spitballs, the BBs rolled down classroom aisles, the back talk to pathetic teachers for whom he should have been able to find some human sympathy, the muted violence of clashes in the school yard, the out-and-out violence of clashes outside the school boundaries, books tossed away, typewriters hurled through open windows…Has it been a distraction that all of those old memories of his own time as a student and now and then some ideas about life and education conjured up by spending time again in school have risen to the surface to share the light with his reporting about this school? He hopes not, because he can't find a way to separate his impressions from his emotions and memories, all of these things that he carries in his backpack wherever he goes. His own school days long ago ended, both his parents dead, his own children living their own lives around the country, and yet the memories persist, so that he can feel right now in this moment under the sun the cold sinking sensation in his blood that came—comes?—with the awareness that his mother might not pick him up after school, or that among these school children now lining up in the hallways on the various floors of the school, preparing their entrances for the Friendship Day festival, might stand his firstborn, his lean young elementary body rippling with the anticipation of performing his song for his (estranged) father and mother.

While flashing back in his mind to these early days, the pilgrim has also been watching with his present eye the arrival of parents, many with infants in their arms, at the school patio, a hundred of them already, the first ten rows or so of seats now nearly filled and the mozos unfolding more chairs at the rear. From the open upper hallways on three sides of the patio, a buzzing and chirping noise has become audible, as the children, like high-strung racehorses, wait nervously to make their entrances in the program. More and more parents enter the patio from the street, some of them scanning the upper hallways for a glimpse of their children. A hundred and fifty adults seated now and waiting, most of them well-dressed, in the casual leather and denim of the reigning middle-class that extends from the northern California of Marin County all the way here to Playas and the upper reaches of Baja California, but some of them having taken time off from service jobs or physical labor to see their children perform—another twenty or thirty arrive before the pilgrim can even finish his surmise about the class makeup of the parents, or even begin to consider the racial mix of light skin and dark, peninsular Spanish and English and German blood, and the Indian ancestry of the noticeable minority here, reflecting the same mix he had found in the classrooms—Mexico, if not a melting pot then what?

"We're almost ready," says Rafe, coming up to the pilgrim with a large sheaf of papers in one hand and a paper headdress in another. "My students wanted you to have these." He hands the pilgrim the papers, which go into his backpack for reading later on. Rafe's eyes are sparking now, not with tears but with the pleasure of standing on the verge of making these students known to their families. He walks back to his students lined up at the door and the pilgrim turns toward the microphone where Liz Hernández, looking grade-school elegant in a floppy hat and sleek skirt, has just taken her stand.

Two hundred and more adults turn toward her as well. The infants quiet down. A gust of wind shushes into the microphone.

She welcomes everybody—in English. And the show begins, the youngest children marching in first in smart lines, and lining up in front of the audience to sing—in English—about numerous little monkeys standing on a bed and falling off and hitting their heads. They depart and another class takes their place, singing about family trees. A few of the oldest boys commandeer one of the microphones and honk, off-key, above the other voices, then fade away as their teacher polices the rows. Twenty minutes of more classes and more songs. Now the next to the oldest, singing that same "Arthur's Theme" that has echoed through both lower and upper school all week.

And I say hey!
HEY!
What a wonderful kind of day!

Everybody's singing, all the students in front of us, and all the teachers, and it is a wonderful kind of day, to participate in this, to witness this, a day to be a child in arms and a day to be a parent and a day to be a teacher and a day to be a student as now the rest of the lower school classes return to the patio, and, of course, the pilgrim looks around, somehow hoping to see his own children, small again, rushing toward him out of the mass of kids in their sweaters and jumpers, from the smallest preschoolers to the rangiest, wisest upper levels, where the boys already have sparks in their eyes though most of them cannot imagine for what, and the dark hair on the Indian girls glows like black gold in the sun, and red hair seems to turn to flame as it blows in the wind and the palest of the pale seem like rare marsh birds about to take flight. Flocks of students, yes! The parents surrounded, the chairs surrounded, the teachers enveloped, the pilgrim, leaning against a pillar, nearly engulfed as the flow increases, dozens and dozens and scores and scores, an ocean of students heaving and surging around him, immersing the patio with their souls and energy and joy beneath the eye of the hot, yellow sun in the sky above Playas, overwhelming any urge that anyone here might have to get them in order, to discipline them or convert them or teach them, not at this moment, not in this instant when they seem like the raw evolving stuff of nature, Mexico's wealth, a gene pool beyond reckoning, and the vital fulcrum on which will move the levers that will change us all.

6—Homework

It's been a long day for Jovanna Venegas, starting out as she did so early in her room in the house in Bonita, sitting in her upper-school class all morning and on into the early afternoon, but now, as usual, the assistant from her father's photography studio has driven over to Playas to pick her up and drive her to the San Ysidro port of entry where they park and walk up the long stairs and across the front of the border station buildings and down the stairs and into the pedestrian crossing building. This is the way to cross, so much quicker than sitting in a car in the long lines of cars in the hot, yellow sun of mid-afternoon.

It's not a long walk, but the day has grown rather warm considering how cool it was in the early morning, and yellow light reflecting off the roadway and the cars seems tarnished and weighs on her head and shoulders. Jovanna's book bag is crammed with texts and homework assignments, and she's a little tired. The weekend lies ahead. So she's just taking things one step at a time, one day at a time, the only way good students do it, and though she has that homework she enjoys solving the problems and enjoys writing the sentences and the essays and enjoys the praise from her teachers when she turns her work in.

Sometimes her parents wonder about her future. Who knows what she will do with her life to come? One sister in Mexico, another who's a photographer in New York City, of all distant places. Her father is quite sure she'll go to a California university. And after that? She might eventually stay north of the border, her English is so good, right now just about as perfect as any eleven-year-old's in any state of the union can be, or she might stay in Mexico and use her English and other studies to good advantage in the Mexico of the new century. But that's not a quandary, scarcely even a question right now at the end of the school week, and as she rushes up to her waiting mother on the U.S. side of the INS turnstiles, she's thinking of nothing perhaps except just how nice it is to be going home.

Or so the pilgrim meditates, sitting in his car while the hot yellow sun heats up the air all around him, and the traffic is not moving at all on the Tijuana side of the border crossing. He himself is quite exhausted after a week at school, though not so tired that he can't take the time to think back on the small events of the week and see how for many of the students, the smallest things will eventually build into the largest. That is the way education works, yes, and though he himself was not a very good student for a very long while he has seen the best things happen in the minds and hearts of his own children when they were still in school, and he's quite sure these things will happen for the kids at Colegio Inglés who work hard and when they're speaking English think in English.

But there's so much more to education than just thinking, of course. The care and humane affection that Rafe Enríquez shows for his students, what sort of intellect can make up for that if it's lacking? Rafe—his face comes back to the pilgrim, and he goes to his backpack to try and find that envelope that the young teacher had passed to him a few hours before. And here it is, and it holds nearly twenty hand drawn and lettered Valentine's cards! All of them say on the front "thank you for coming to our school," with the word "coming" often given an extra *m*. Inside, the students write their names and their favorite subjects. Evelyn Abigail González Gómez likes art and English and P.E. while what Gerarde likes most "is reces for is very cool and I like the girls from the school they are beutiful," and Gaby likes English and Spanish and art, and Rosalba likes math class "because is cool," and Victor likes "the uniform and the class," and Norberto's "clas favorite is art," and María del Mar likes English and "espanich," and on and on, the pleasure and hope mixed with the crudity and lack of uniform quality.

The evidence shows that these fourth graders have a long way to go, but whatever their level, their grasp or lack of it, they are on their way, and teachers like Liz Hernández and Ms. Ivy and Rafe and Mr. Dan are giving their best efforts, heart and soul, to help them, and most of them will move toward a different life from the one they might have had without this school, and many of them are heading in this same direction as the pilgrim, as the traffic suddenly unjams and begins to roll forward, north, over the border, into San Diego County and the rest of California beyond, and eight or ten or fifteen years from now you may know them. They will work for you, they will work with you, they will become your bosses and colleagues and friends, and marry you or your children, and you will sing with them in English, and it will, take a good guess, yes, it will only be a pleasure.

Originally published in the San Diego Reader

THE MEXICAN RABBI

1—*The Story of Hernando Alonso*

Ciudad de México, 1528—A bell clangs and he, with the great difficulty of an old man with stiff limbs and creaking bones, sits up in the dark, awakened from a sleep that had taken him far away from the high stink of his own urine and the stench of his own ordure in the far corner of the cell, away from the shouts and cries of madness and pain in the night.

Hernando Alonso is back.

He had been dreaming a strange and fluent dream, an excursion to far places to which he had found himself flying like a bird, at one point soaring over an entire fleet of brigantines and knowing, even as he looked down, that it had been his own armada, the very ships that had so long ago carried him and all of the troops of Hernán Cortés from Hispania to Cuba and then to the shores of this territory that he had called home for nearly ten years.

There had been battles along the way, and there had been forests, and the conquerors on horseback had won the battles, with some help from tribes angry with the ruling Aztecs, and, after winning, the soldiers had cut down many trees so that the plain would look more like home and set the pigs to rooting which had the double effect of feeding the troops and destroying more trees. In the rising noise of the prison in early morning he could still hear the barks and screams of those early wars.

He had been born in Condado de Niebla and grew up in Cádiz, a city of water and sails, one of three sons of a carpenter named Joseph.

How ironic, yes! The same name as the father of the Savior. And it was his father who had taught him beginning at an early age his trade, carpentry, and then working with metal so that he had become a smithy. And initiated him into the secret religion of their forefathers, one of whose rules was that he should eat no pork.

The old rules had made for a lot of trouble in the old land. The time in which Hernando Alonso grew into manhood was filled with stories of funeral pyres piled with burning logs and Jews on fire! Not until he was in his thirties, still unmarried, his father having died and left him the shop and the tools, one of his brothers disappeared in the middle of a voyage to Africa, the other brother a success in the ships-handling trade, that good news arrived. It came from across the water. An expedition mounted by the Crown had returned with word about New Lands, new territories on the other side of the great ocean.

Ever since Hernando had been a small child he had listened avidly to the stories of the voyages around the coast of Africa made by Portuguese explorers, and then after he came into his manhood to news of the Spanish voyages to the New World. In his heart, he felt a deep longing, more like a tingling that worked through his chest when he thought such things, to sail away from this place of subterfuge, silence, and the fearful flames.

But in the end, it hadn't been his heart that had taken him across the sea to the New World; it had been his hands. When the call went out along the docks, he was a man in mid-age but still it seemed natural for him to sign up as a ship's carpenter on the royal expedition led by Hernán Cortés. His brother had known for years the ship's captain who would pilot one of the galleons in Cortés's fleet and had made it possible for Hernando to sail west with the would-be conquerors. Gonzalo stood weeping at the dockside and Hernando's own eyes turned wet, but he did not let the tears flow, fearful that the rough sailors who passed along the rail would take it as a sign of weakness. When the land sank down beneath the waters to the east, a large part of his heart felt that it was sinking, too.

The passage was rough, the ships meeting awful, heaving seas. Alonso, along with many others, suffered moments of cold and disabling fear. With the winds blowing hard and the great waves breaking across the bows of the brigantine, he dropped to the planking and put his hands to his face, saying quietly, "Please, Dear Lord, Lord of Abraham and Isaac, spare me a watery death! Oh, spare me, spare me, I pray You." And then, just to be sure, he would reach for the crucifix that he wore about his thick neck and hold it cupped in his hands as the salt waves broke over his feet. The wind howled about the tops of the mast, the voice of evil hell-hounds chasing after his soul.

"Spare me, Oh, Lord," Alonso prayed, "and I will dedicate my life to the duties of your Holy Person."

Hernando Alonso is the first Jew to have his presence in the New World set down in a historical record. Some historians speculate that other Jews came as Hernando Alonso did, on board one of the Spanish oceangoing ships—a few of them, it is presumed, with the early expeditions of Columbus and others with Cortés's fleet, but Alonso is the first to be noted. There are also some romantic-minded interpreters of history who would argue that Columbus himself was a hidden Jew, but no one has ever proved this. As for Hernando Alonso, he had signed on as a ship's carpenter. But once the need became apparent, during the year of war between the Spaniards and the various eastern Mexican tribes, he put to use his skill as a blacksmith, repairing the steel of weapons, reshoeing the horses so necessary to the victories over the Indians.

On the night of the great battle in the city in the middle of the lake against the Aztec rulers of Tenochtitlán, the night the Mexicans have come to call the Noche Triste, Hernando Alonso's talents served the army well. The ship's carpenter oversaw the construction of the thirteen bridges to the city so that the Spanish troops could enter in force. He had crossed the main bridge himself just behind the archers (and a few days later he was present in the crowd of troops when they heard that Moctezuma, the Indian King and God, now a captive of the Spaniards, had died, killed by a stone thrown by one of his own people).

For his part in the conquest of the Aztec capital, Alonso was awarded land and cattle and some Indian captives to be used as slaves. These he set to work clearing a ranch where he raised imported cattle and, forgive him, Oh, God of Abraham and Isaac, hogs for sale to the army for meat. His brother had come to join him. Only two years after Hernando had sailed for the New World, the Spanish Court issued the Edict of 1523, forbidding Jews, Moors, or other heretics from taking up residence in New Spain.

So his brother had used a forged document and his friendship with another sea captain to gain entry to these new lands under the name of Morales.

Morales: "And do they know you are a Jew?"

Alonso: "I am what I am. I have never hidden anything. I believe what I believe and I have gone to mass in the church that we have built on the place where the Aztec temple stood."

Morales: "It is a crime for a Jew to cross the border into New Spain. We are both criminals in the eyes of the Crown."

Alonso: "I have helped the Crown win mighty victories."

Morales: "You raise swine for the soldiers of the Crown. And in turn they would call you a hog."

Alonso: "No one calls me anything but my own name."

After the victory Mass that had been served in that church where the pagan temple had stood, few of the old soldiers attended. But Alonso became enamored of one of his female slaves and freed her and married her in this same church. His first child was baptized there, although when he returned home after the ceremony, Hernando, much to the dismay of his wife, who feared that one of servants would see him, dipped his fingers in wine, splashed it on his child's brow, and then drank the rest of the wine in the cup. Staring down at the child's naked body, he thanked the old Hebrew God that a daughter had come to him instead of a son, because he did not have to worry about the problem of circumcision. If the child had been a boy, would he, Hernando, have to have made the cut himself? No, no, he would have asked his brother. But would he have done it?

Nights on the ranch on the high plateau, skies filled with burning stars, the sound of the animals lowing in the corrals—he thought himself so fortunate that he had removed himself from the turmoil back home. Once the army had defeated the Indians here, a great calm had settled over the center of the territory. He himself had given all of his own servants their freedom, all of them staying on to work at the ranch. But when he and his wife strolled in the center of the city he noticed the conquerors, turning fat and grey some half dozen years after the end of the war, shouting at Indians, kicking at them, in one instance punching one to the ground for not getting out of the way quickly enough. He had come to love his wife, and it disturbed him to see her fellow Indians, her family, treated in such a manner.

But there was nothing he could do except behave in the best way he knew how toward his own servants. In the quiet of their bed he would tell her stories from the Five Books of Moses, stories he had learned as a child, and gradually she understood that though they both attended mass, he still valued the old ceremonies of the Jews. Although the news from Spain had it that the Inquisition's fires were burning brightly, fed by the bodies of unrepentant Jews, here on the high plateau of Mexico Alonso felt so distant from such matters that he scarcely gave it a thought. Here was a place where he could grow old in peace. The Franciscans were avidly attending to the business of converting the Indians. They didn't seem to have time to worry about the faith of the old soldiers and their retinues.

When the second child came, again he dipped his fingers in wine and dripped some of the liquid onto the girl's forehead—oh, yes, Thank the Lord, another girl!—saying some old but newly recollected words in the Ladino tongue. Other memories jittered flamelike in his mind. One Sunday just before mass, with his wife in her monthlies, he told her to stay at home.

"Señora," he is reported to have said, "in your present condition thou wouldst profane the Church."

His wife replied, "These are old ceremonies of the Jews which are not observed now that we have adopted the evangelical grace…"

When the priest inquired about her, leaning down to pat one of the children on the head, Alonso said, "She is ill." It became his custom, asking her to stay away from Mass when she was in that condition. Whether or not the priest noticed, he never said anything more about it.

Another few years went by, all those ink-black nights passing beneath the hot and burning stars, the children grew, he and his brother increased their cattle and swine herds ten-fold. Alonso had competition in the bidding but the city council recognized his seniority by accepting his bids over some lower proposals. It didn't hurt that the acting governor of New Spain was an old shipmate, Alonso de Estrada.

Did his rivals speak badly of him? Did they make clear that they knew he was a secret Jew and thus undeserving of special privilege? It didn't matter to him. He was getting to be an old man and thought that he deserved such deference. Think back to the Noche Triste and how it might have been if he hadn't built those bridges to the center of the city. Now and then he would see his old commander at Mass. The greying warrior looked over at him, as if to ask, Why does a Hebrew man like yourself suffer this inscrutable pageantry? Old soldiers still kept up their brawling in the taverns and the streets, sometimes even right up to the steps of the churches. The priests spoke to Cortés, but he pleaded for his men. Would the Church itself be here in Mexico without these soldiers?

And then came the spring of 1528, and the arrival in the city of the Dominican friar San Vicente de María, sent to Mexico to act in all matters against the Faith as well as to establish the first monasteries. A number of conquistadores were hauled in before a church tribunal to answer for blasphemies and other insults. Still, Hernando Alonso did not worry about himself because his old commander would look after him. Then in May Cortés returned to Spain to plead some grievances before the Crown and Alonso was left without a protector.

It didn't take long before they came for him in the night, leaving behind his sobbing wife and sleeping children. His priest-confessor stood to one side while a Dominican friar conducted the proceedings. The charges against him were composed of three counts: 1) That his children were baptized twice, once by a Franciscan friar and then again "according to the ritual of the law of Moses." 2) That he refused to permit his wife to attend Mass when she was having her menstrual period. 3) The third charge: a witness, one of his own former slaves whom he had freed, stated that Alonso poured water over the head of one of his children and then drank the water in mockery of baptism. According to the records of the archives of the Mexican Inquisition, the witness stated also that Alonso sang a psalm that referred to Israel's Lord God of Egypt, "o una cosa de esta manera..." Thus he was found guilty of "Judaizing," the punishment for which was death by fire. Days went by and then his brother was thrown into the same cell with him.

"The fire that burned in Spain," Gonzalo said. "It has almost caught up with us."

"But why?" Alonso asked. "I have made a good life here and I have done good things for the territory."

"It is a matter of blood," his brother said.

"Do they want blood? I'll give them some of my blood in exchange for life."

"Our blood is no good to them," his brother said. "They say it is different from theirs. It sullies their veins. They want to purify the bloodlines of New Spain just as they have in the old country."

"Why is our blood impure?" Alonso said. "Why?" he said when they came for him on the last morning and slipped the ritual garment over his head. He walked slowly along the route to the pyre, his head bowed with that question weighing heavily on his mind. Surely they were not going to execute him just for being who he was? He, who had crossed the ocean sea border to help defeat the pagan Aztec? And my children, my children, what of them, what will become of them? Such questions haunted him until the very instant that he smelled his own flesh burning.

2—More Fuel for the Flames

Hernando Alonso was the first Mexican Jew, and, as the records of the Mexican Inquisition reveal, the first Jew to be killed in the New World. But not the last. By the end of the sixteenth century, so-called conversos, or people with Jewish family roots who converted to Catholicism, were going to the fires with some regularity in the Kingdom of New Spain, with the greatest number of people accused as Jews burned at the stake in the Great Auto de Fe of 1649. Merchants, monks, pharmacists, doctors, actors, weavers, constables, jewelers, shoemakers, handymen, mostly men, some women, nearly a hundred in number. According to the records of the time, one woman was the sister of a Jesuit priest and mother of a Dominican monk. As historian Judith Elkin has written, though the woman was raised in a Catholic household and raised her own children as Catholic, she still had not sufficient warranty that as a converso she could take her place in Mexican society.

From the lowest to the highest in society, few escaped the scrutiny of the Inquisition. Take the case of Luis de Carvajal y de la Cueva, the first governor of the province of Nuevo Leon, recently glorified in the San Diego Opera production of *The Conquistador*. Carvajal was not a Jew, nor were his parents, though his maternal grandmother and his wife were Jewesses. While never found guilty of being Jewish, he was convicted by the tribunal for not reporting to them that his nephews and niece observed Jewish rites. As historian Samuel Liebman has noted, their Judaism stemmed from their father, and their mother adopted or was converted to Judaism by her husband. Dishonored, stripped of rank and office, Carvajal escaped the flames but died in jail. Others like him went to prison for extended terms or spent years as galley slaves, their lives ripped asunder by the wrath of the Inquisitors whose task, as they saw it, was to establish the purity of the bloodlines of the Kingdom. The chemistry of the Inquisition seemed apt. Flames were a good instrument for purification. Those who escaped into the countryside or left for the north were burned in effigy. Others who had died in their cells before they could be turned over to the secular authorities for execution had their bones disinterred and roasted in the pyres, their names inscribed on the church walls and in church ledgers, which is how we have such a precise record of just how many Jews went up in flames: Alonso, Carvajal, Castro, Fernández, García, Gómez, González, León, López, Machado, Méndez, Núñez, Paz, Peña, Pereira, Perez, Rodríguez, Rosa, Suárez, Tinoco, Torres, Villegas, Zarate. A few of the names of the hordes of so-called crypto-Jews or hidden Jews or Judaizers of the New World who went to their deaths by fire. On the same locations where once the Aztecs sacrificed thousands of victims to their old gods, the Church now burned hundreds of old believers for the sake of the new God.

3—A Young Man with a Long Beard

In Tijuana, at the Centro Social Israelita, the compound that houses the local Orthodox sanctuary, fears of such inquisitions turn otherwise sound minds toward paranoia four hundred years after the fact. The façade of the center, located on a narrow one-way street just south of the Tijuana business district where the neighbors include the local Lions Club, a liquor store, and second-class motels, is drab and unobtrusive, masking, in typical Mexican fashion, the complex behind it. Beneath the green awning of the entryway is the only sign out of the ordinary in this Catholic neighborhood: a small cardboard Star of David taped behind the glass door. When I visited there earlier this spring, the governing board of Tijuana's Jewish Center seemed to be torn between welcoming an inquiring journalist and hiding themselves from the public eye.

The rabbi himself, an earnest young man all of twenty-five who is on his first pastoral assignment, betrayed no fear whatsoever. His name is Mendel Polichenko, and he is a fresh-eyed fellow born in Argentina, educated in Israel and New York, and married to an Orthodox girl from a rabbinical family of eleven children whose sombre dress can't hide her still girlish energy and expectations. Rabbi Polichenko belongs to the Chabad movement, the zealous Orthodox sect—some call it a cult—with its center in the Crown Heights section of Brooklyn where for many decades its leader (most revered him as their Messiah) the late Rabbi Schneerson, held sway. When I met Rabbi Polichenko on a weekday, dressed as he was in a dark blue doublebreasted blazer and slacks, his long dark beard reaching down over the knot of his necktie, he might have been a first-year graduate student about to take a deep breath, check the knot in his tie, and plunge into a room to teach his first class in religion. On the Sabbath, he appeared in the traditional long coat and made the very picture of a youthful Orthodox leader, certainly someone whom the friars of the Inquisition could never have imagined flourishing on Mexican soil.

Had he ever held fears about revealing his Jewishness in Tijuana? Never, he replied. Was he worried about Mexican anti-Semitism? Not at all, he said. Growing up in Buenos Aires, he explained, he was sometimes "made aware" of being Jewish when he went out on the street. But most of his life there he spent within the silk-lined ghetto of the thriving Jewish community. His own parents, immigrants from Eastern Europe, crossed a number of borders to reach the New World, but aside from his own study visits to Israel, Polichenko has spent most of his time in North America.

He first arrived in Tijuana as part of a Chabad internship while he was still a rabbinical student. For two summers, he assisted in the life of the center, which had been without a regular spiritual leader for some years. After his ordination, he returned to work full time for the Jews of this hectic border city, now administered by the opposition, Catholic-oriented PAN, the last place in the West where you might expect to see the figure of an Old World rabbi, broad-brimmed hat, long coat, his devoted wife at his side, walking along the roadway while dented, vintage Chevys and Oldsmobiles roared past, spraying noxious exhaust.

4—Reaching for America

It is a bit of an anomaly, if not a miracle, that Rabbi Polichenko is the current spiritual leader of the majority of the Jews in Tijuana. It's also really quite amazing that the center has held together for as long as it has, considering the strains upon its membership and its peculiar location. Aside from an occasional Jewish businessman who came to Baja California from north of the border, Tijuana's Jewish community was virtually nonexistent until the end of World War II. As for the country at large, a first wave of Jewish immigrants arrived in Mexico from Eastern

Europe after the Napoleonic Wars and then in a second wave around the turn of the century. The majority of these people had the United States in mind as their ultimate destination; most of them had to settle in Latin America. As one Jewish Mexican social psychologist told me, surveying the scene below from the seventeenth floor of his Mexico City office building, "My father came here from Poland as poor as any of the peasants in those shanties down below. What did he know? He wanted to come to America and spent his last money for the passage. And he reached America—but it was South America. The port where he landed was Veracruz. He sold pots and pans in the streets and eventually came to Mexico City. There he met my mother, who was also born in Eastern Europe."

From Mexico to Argentina, tens of thousands of Old Country Jews arrived to work as itinerant peddlers and shopkeepers, making new families in the relatively liberal atmosphere of the New World. For many of the Ashkenazim, the Jews of Eastern European origin who now number about 60 percent of the community, Mexico was regarded at first as a way station on the route to North America. For the Sephardim, the Jews of Mediterranean origin who arrived from Turkey, Bulgaria, Lebanon, and Syria, Mexico seemed more hospitable with respect to both climate and language.

Settling mainly in Mexico City and Guadalajara, these Jewish emigrants numbered approximately eight thousand between 1905 and 1910, with another surge of immigration between the World Wars that added another fifteen thousand people to the Jewish community of Mexico. Many Jews from Germany, Russia, Poland, and Hungary (the four main Ashkenazi communities), especially those trained in various crafts, found no market for those occupations and adapted their skills to the country's needs. They parlayed small beginnings into large entrepreneurships in the manufacturing world.

The father of my social-psychologist friend, for example, went in his lifetime from peddler to warehouseman to warehouse owner.

A lot of the Sephardim entered the clothing trades, moving from jobs as machine workers to manufacturers. Members of the Zaga family of Mexico City are a case in point, progressing from immigrants to a household name in one generation by virtue of their widely advertised men's shirts.

About 60 percent of the economically active Jews in the large Mexico City population entered into the manufacture and sales of footwear, underwear, men's clothing and paper products. Some 25 percent produce other staples such as furniture, textiles, and electrical appliances. The remaining 15 percent include professionals, clerks, and civil servants. All the newcomers followed the tradition of the closely knit, self-helping family which they had brought along with their baggage. With as much skill and tenacity as they applied to the burgeoning business world, they also organized the Jewish community.

Each geographical and tribal group established its own *kehillah*, the democratically constituted central body of the community. When the Ashkenazim in Mexico City set up the Nichde Israel about fifty years ago, Yiddish was their preferred language most of the time. The German and Hungarian immigrants founded two different *kehillot*, the Hatikva Menorah and the Emuna; their respective mother tongues were spoken there. The Sephardim created the Union Sefaradi de Mexico, and the Arabic-speaking group divided according to countries of origin, with Jews from Damascus, Syria, in one *kehillah* and those from Aleppo, Turkey, in the other.

These organizations helped develop an extensive Jewish school system which since the 1920s has provided a fully rounded program in religious as well as secular subjects from elementary through high school levels. About 65 percent of

Mexican Jewish children currently attend these schools. The curriculum includes secular subjects prescribed by the Ministry of Education and Jewish studies, usually in an equally balanced combination. By means of this extensive educational network, the Jewish community succeeded in passing on its heritage to each succeeding generation.

They achieved this in the face of some difficult social and psychological barriers. As historian Judith Elkin has written, these people were "triple strangers" in Mexico, by dint of their religion, their ethnic origin, and their historical experience. However, over the decades of their adjustment and settlement, their lives were affected by distinctively Mexican factors. Of major importance are laws passed in the wake of Mexico's liberation early in the nineteenth century from Spanish rule, which bar the foreign-born and their offspring from elected political office and other key posts, such as rectorships in universities. One result has been that Mexican Jews have expressed themselves politically almost solely *within* their community, first creating potent bureaucracies for the synagogues and other institutions, and then organizing central bodies. Today the Comité Central Israelita de México, originally the Committee for Refugees, founded in 1938, reflects the kaleidoscope of nationalities and religious practices and represents Mexican Jewry as a whole to the government, other Jewish organizations, and the world outside.

Because Mexico's liberal modern constitution decrees separation of church and state, the Jews were not confronted with overt, Church-generated anti-Semitism, as has been the case in other Latin American countries. But anti-Semitism still exists at the popular level. The brisk sales of such violently anti-Jewish publications as *The Protocols of the Elders of Zion*, which appear on newsstands alongside pornographic publications and sports papers, attest to this. Although the Jews, going from peddlers to manufacturers, played a noticeable role in the industrialization and modernization of twentieth-century Mexico, when the Depression hit and the price of silver dropped, they were treated as foreigners. For instance, on March 27, 1931, during the annual "Day of Commerce" parade in Mexico City, Jewish merchants were forced out of the Lagunilla Market.

"Buy from Mexicans—Boycott Jews!"

That was the motto of the day.

Anti-Semitic sentiment in Mexico came to a head during the late thirties and on into the war years as nationalism sometimes turned to anti-foreign sentiment. Nationalists grouped the Jews with outsiders. Anti-Jewish propaganda fostered by the German diplomatic corps encouraged this line of attack.

DAILY GLOBE intelube londres presse collect following yesterdays
headcoming antisemitic campaign mexpress propetition
se tee emma mexworkers
confederation proexpulsion exmexico quote small
jewish textile manufacturers
unquote twas learned today per-reliable source that
german legation mexcity
actively behind the campaign etstatement that legation
gone length sending
antisemitic propaganda mexdept interiorwards borne out
propamphlet possession
local newspaperman stop pamphlet asserts jews influence
unfavourably any
country they live etemphasises quote their belief absolute
power etthat they gain
their ends without conscience or consideration unquote stop...

We get some of the flavor of this trying period in the cable sent by Hugh Firmin, a British citizen, working as a news stringer in Mexico, in Malcolm Lowry's novel *Under the Volcano* set in Mexico in 1938. In the streets and in the cantinas, as Lowry depicts the time, the accusations combined xenophobia with drunken delusions. "You no wrider," says a rural police chief, taking Lowry's main character by the throat. "You Al Capon. You a Jew chingao…"

5—"A New Sort of Ghetto"

In the minds of the central Jewish community in post–World War II Mexico City, Baja California was the last frontier, a place wide open for the tough-minded entrepreneur where Jews were unknown and conventional biases might fall away. However, two Jewish businessmen, one arriving from the North, the other Mexican-born, had already played a prominent role in the development of this territory. Just after the American Civil War, at a time when Mexicali did not exist, and Tijuana was still a ranch, a Polish-born, polyglot, Anaheim resident named Louis Mendelson, a veteran of the Fourth Missouri Volunteers, almost single-handedly blazed a trail in this new territory. Mendelson, already a successful California lumber yard owner, went south when he heard the news of a gold rush in the San Rafael Valley, about twenty-five miles east of Ensenada. There he opened a general store and quickly established himself as one of Baja California del Norte's most prominent residents, buying a part-ownership of the major gold mine, raising sheep, marrying Carmen Lamadrid, a young woman from a local family, and entering local politics in Real del Castillo, the mining town that became the new capital of the region.

Mendelson made traversing the nearby border a way of life, often traveling north to see family and to use his good knowledge of Hebrew while officiating at Sabbath services at Congregation Beth Israel, the small Jewish congregation that was founded in San Diego in 1861, which was often without a regular rabbi. As historian Donald Chaput reports, as early as 1882, Louis Mendelson traveled up from Baja and his brother Max Mendelson came down from San Juan Capistrano and together they led the High Holy Day services. By the time the San Rafael Valley gold mine began to fail, Mendelson had become Attorney-General of Baja, serving at the same time as an agent for the Connecticut-based, London-financed International Company, the foreign developers of the region. He worked with and eventually took over from another Jew, the Mexican-born Max Bernstein who was employed by the company from 1886 into the 1890s. Mendelson later turned his acquired legal expertise to good use in a successful customs brokerage in San Diego. He kept an office on the docks at 1345 G Street and a residence at 1335 Eighteenth Street where he spent the last several decades of his life. Mendelson died in a Los Angeles hospital in 1908, and was buried in L.A., but his wife, Carmen Lamadrid Mendelson, remained in San Diego until her death in 1948 at the age of eighty-one.

To cite one notable contemporary example of Jewish emigration to Baja, the father of well-known Tijuana businessman José Galicot—a Jew of Turkish descent—worked as a peddler in the state of Chihuahua before moving his young family to Tijuana in the late 1940s. Tijuana, currently at more than a million people, had a population then of only about twenty thousand. One of the most prominent forces in the town at the time of the arrival of the Galicots was a Jewish chemist named Leon Blum. Blum and a few other friends organized concerts and exhibitions of the work of local artists, and established a Jewish social club called the Mogen David or Star of David Club and later the Hatikvah Club, after the national anthem of the state of Israel, clubs which evolved into the present Centro Social Israelita.

Another classic example is that of the Goldsteins, founders and owners of Dorians Department Store. The elder Goldstein, born in Rumania, survived internment in a Nazi concentration camp and after spending some time at the end of the war in Italy and Marseilles arrived in Tijuana in the late 1940s and sold wristwatches on the street. His son Gregorio, Jr., was born in Tijuana and, in what is not an untypical story for many young Tijuana-born Jews, traveled across the border to attend high school and college in San Diego. He met his wife, a Jewish girl from Guadalajara, while working as a counsellor at the Jewish summer camp established by the Centro's religious leader at the time, Max Furmansky, and went into the family business.

The Jewish community of Mexico City stabilized in this period at a level of about thirty-seven thousand, with about another eight hundred to a thousand or so in Guadalajara, a similar number in Monterrey and then another hundred or thereabouts in Acapulco. For twenty years the Jewish community in Tijuana absorbed numerous families, emigrating from these places, and the families already in place produced a second generation. As Gregorio Goldstein, Jr., puts it, "Tijuana in those days was a magnet for people who wanted good business opportunities." The Jewish community grew as the city grew, as Jewish businessmen put their savings and new loans into the development of some of Tijuana's most visible commercial enterprises, such as Dorian's and the Sarah's chain, ushering in a golden era for the Jews of Tijuana.

Businessmen like José Galicot were quite visible and active in local clubs and charities, and kept up good relations with the local bishop. Not even Mexico's notorious support for the 1975 United Nations Resolution equating Zionism with racism put much of a dent in the life of Jewish Tijuanians. For most of the Jews living there the city became for a while, in Galicot's words, "a new sort of ghetto," a magical, privileged place, with the proximity of San Diego, where many Jewish families had, as Galicot calls it, a "nest" to which they could retreat for vacations or for business, acting as a good influence on relations between Catholics and Jews. Business was good, and the community grew in size, according to most estimates, to somewhere between a hundred and fifty and a little over two hundred families, a number of them living on the U.S. side of the border and traveling down to Tijuana every day, all of them committed, nonetheless, to the well-being of the Tijuana Centro.

There were, of course, a few problems, and it was precisely that same proximity to San Diego that seemed to create some of them. The Centro just couldn't seem to find a spiritual leader who wanted to settle here. Rabbis came and went, mainly visitors from the north. It wasn't until the early seventies that Max Furmansky arrived from Buenos Aires with his family to live here and lead the congregation. Furmansky was a Conservative Jew rather than Orthodox, and he was not an ordained rabbi but was trained as a cantor to lead the musical parts of the Sabbath services. Despite the fact that most of the families in place came from Orthodox backgrounds, they welcomed a man who was willing to make the commitment to stay.

Furmansky went to work, leading the Sabbath services, organizing classes in Jewish law and history for the children in the community and inaugurating a month-long Jewish summer camp that enrolled hundreds of children from Mexico City and Guadalajara as well as local Jewish kids, housing the visitors in local homes. The camp conducted numerous trips north across the border to such attractions as Sea World, and a week of camping in the countryside of Baja California. Furmansky's own son, Josef, now a successful San Diego software entrepreneur, remembers his first four years in Tijuana as "a beautiful time," with the Jewish community center as the focal point of his activity. In 1977, Furmansky moved his family to San Diego, but remained at the head of the congregation, and young Josef, though he now attended Hebrew Day School in San Diego, traveled with his father nearly every day to the Tijuana center where he studied martial arts and played soccer on the Jewish team. Even in the heat of the playing field where the Jews went head to head against Catholic teams, he claims that he never heard any anti-Semitic slurs. This, and a roof over the family and food on the table, for a Jew accounts as a sort of paradise.

6—Turmoil in Paradise

The real turmoil in the Jewish community here came from within. As business conditions improved in Tijuana from the end of the Second World War on, there had been a regular influx of families from Mexico City and Guadalajara, and a number of these people were of Sephardic origin.

The Sephardim, Jews of Mediterranean and Middle Eastern origin, are the direct descendants of the original tribes of Israel and their locale has stretched from the cities and deserts of old Persia and Syria (and some having migrated as far east as India) to the antique cities of Italy, Greece, and Spain. Physiologically they resemble their Arab cousins in facial features, hair, and skin coloring. The Jews of the Kingdom of Spain were Sephardic Jews who, along with the Moors, formed two thirds of the great religious triad of the Golden Age of Iberian culture. The Ashkenazim also claim direct descent from the original Israelites, but physically they seem distinct from the Sephardim, and their origins are lost in the cloudy era of the early Middle Ages. How to account for the advent of Jewish peddlers and merchants in the Kingdom of Old Russia in the eleventh and twelfth centuries? The most imaginative and compelling argument comes from the late European writer Arthur Koestler who speculated that these Jews were descended from the Central Asian tribe called the Khazars who, when their ruler converted to Judaism in the tenth century AD, converted along with him.

Orthodox Jews don't like this version of their origins, and most dismiss it out of hand. In the current context of the debate in Israel about Jewish identity—with the ruling Orthodox rabbis asserting that only an Orthodox conversion makes for a "real" Jew, thus excluding from the community all of those converts who have undergone conversion under the auspices of Conservative rabbis—it nettles even more. But even before the current debate the schism between Ashkenazim and Sephardim caused quite a bit of political trouble in the state of Israel, with political parties organizing along these inter-ethnic lines, and the dark-complected Sephardim sometimes claiming racial discrimination by the European Ashkenazism.

Because of the historical separation of the Sephardic Jews from the Ashkenazim, the Sephardic religious service evolved in some distinctive ways from the services of the other community. This is most pronounced in the melodies used to sing certain prayers. For the Jews of Mexico City, where each of the groups prayed in their separate ways, such distinctions never proved to be points of contention. In the early 1980s a Sephardic family named Adato moved from Mexico City to Tijuana and having no choice about where to pray joined the Centro, starting a small war over the religious practice of the Sabbath service. They began a campaign for separate religious services at the Centro for Sephardim that tore the community apart. By the time the Adatos moved back to Mexico City, the once numerous Jewish community of the Centro was reduced to about fifty or sixty families and without a regular spiritual leader.

It wasn't just the squabble between the Sephardic Jews and the Ashkenazi Jews that led to the shrinkage of the Centro's membership. In a dispute over his contract, Max Furmansky resigned from his post as spiritual head of the congregation, leaving the community without a regular religious guide for many years. The economy was also a force in the dissolution of the Tijuana Centro. A major devaluation of the peso sent a number of prominent Jewish Mexican Tijuana families north across the border in order to establish themselves in the more stable U.S. economy. Just as commuting back and forth from Tijuana to San Diego has become a way of life for more than fifty thousand Mexican service workers, commuting in the opposite direction became the rule for many Jewish Mexican businessmen. More than half of the Centro's congregants have moved to San Diego County, and many of these, while keeping some affiliation with the Centro, have joined other congregations in their new California home.

That's why you can hear so much Spanish spoken at the Conservative Temple Adath Ami in Mission Valley. Nearly half the congregation of the Conservative Temple Adath Ami, led by Argentine-born Rabbi Arnold Kopikis, used to belong to the Centro in Tijuana. Tijuana's drought has led to Adath Ami's deluge. Rabbi Kopikis speaks with pleasure of the way that the Jews who wandered over the border have enriched the religious and social life of his congregation. As for the hopes for the Tijuana Centro's survival, he is not very sanguine. Rabbi Polichenko, for all of his good intentions, is "a nostalgic reminder of the Old World" rather than someone who can hold the rapidly shrinking Tijuana Jewish community intact. "It's not a natural coupling," he explains.

(In fact, rumors have flown as far east as the Jewish community in Mexico City to the effect that some of the exodus from the Centro to San Diego congregations comes in part from the discomfort on the part of some Tijuana Jews with Polichenko's Old World demeanor and approach.)

"When they were in chaos down there," Rabbi Kopikis continued, "Chabad sent help in the person of Rabbi Polichenko. It's holding steady for a while. But how long can they hold out? Their financial resources are not great. They're having a lot of money problems within the Centro, and there's not a big hope for donations the way the Chabad people might have thought. Eventually Chabad will withdraw Polichenko and someone from up here will email the Sabbath service to them down there."

In the past few years the growing disintegration of Mexican middle-class life has led to even further Jewish emigration from Tijuana. Kidnappings are on the rise in the major cities, and while no Jews from Tijuana have yet been the target of such plots, fear of these matters has led to the growth of a strain of cautiousness to the point of paranoia on the part of some members of the Centro.

7—At the Centro Social Israelita

Rabbi Polichenko had been hospitable and forthcoming with me, pleased to take me on a tour of the Centro's facilities. But all of his good cheer could not put a good face on the condition of the compound, its drab classrooms, the large sanctuary whose glaring light suggested more a high school auditorium than an Orthodox synagogue, the bedraggled children's playground, the grass ragged and ungroomed, the small swimming pool a rather pathetic imitation of the grand Olympic-size pool that you find at the glorious Jewish Sports Center in Mexico City. Clearly, there was something lax about the upkeep of these facilities, something that went beyond the possibility that the congregation lacked the funds to maintain the grounds in pristine fashion. On the lower east side of New York City, there are centers like this in the city welfare system, where the barest amount of money is put aside for maintenance so that the city's poor children might have a place to play after school. On the lower east side of New York City there are other places, now abandoned, or turned into Pentecostal churches, where the grandfathers fresh off the boats from the Old World once gathered to say their ancient prayers in the New World air.

But I kept these reservations to myself and was pleased that at the end of our meeting the rabbi invited me to the next day's Sabbath service and the community supper that would follow. Perhaps my first impressions were mistaken and this was a place still full of life rather than a location where slow decay ruled and old traditions had been cast into a corner to waste away from lack of maintenance. Unfortunately I wasn't going to have much chance to look at these matters in the best light. When Rabbi Polichenko had me follow him up the stairs to a meeting room where the board of the congregation was just finishing a session, I was immediately met with great suspicion.

"Do you have any identification?" The woman co-chair of the board—let's call her Mrs. S., since she asked me not to use her name—made this demand as though she were expecting an infiltrator from the Mexican provincial police. A plump and stumpy figure in a plain dress, she stood squarely between me and the other members of the board in the meeting room on the second floor of the Centro. When I explained that my mission was to write a story about the Jewish community of Tijuana her face closed and the board scattered.

The next day, at the approach of the Sabbath, and my next visit to the Centro, Mrs. S. was even more direct and hostile.

"The board met and talked about your story," she said. "We voted that you don't write it."

I had arrived a few hours earlier and had spent the time talking with members of the Centro, some of them Ashkenazi, some of them Sephardic, about their lives in Tijuana, and about the life of the Jewish community here. In what appears to be the dwindling latter years of the Centro, the rift between the two main tribal factions seems to have been repaired, if only by inertia. The young men present seemed dedicated to their religion and their culture. Rabbi Polichenko has obviously been a positive force in the mending of any lingering feuds and the outlook of these fellows. The only complaints from the boys I spoke to had to do with—surprise, surprise—the lack of eligible Jewish women in the community. Some of the boys had studied in Israel and were thinking about going back. Or at least to Los Angeles for a social hour with some Jewish girls up there. Like Orthodox Jews anywhere, these fellows spoke as if they lived on an island, surrounded by gentile waters. Not that they had any problems with their neighbors. It was just their mournful thoughts about dating that came out in the form of laments. Blood! blood! The bloodline had to survive!

I had intended to continue my conversation with these young men after the Friday evening service, but now Mrs. S., the co-chair of the governing board was about to make that impossible.

"So you can come in if you don't write your story," she told me.

"Things don't work that way," I said.

"How do they work?" Mrs. S. said as we stood in the vestibule of the Centro. She stood her ground.

"You're writing this story for who?"

I explained again.

"How much are they paying you?"

"Enough," I said.

"Well, we'll pay you the same amount not to write it," she said.

"Are you offering me a bribe?" I said.

"We'll pay you not to write the story," she said.

"You'll pay me off?"

"Please," she said, "we don't want any stories. It's a bad situation here, people have had death threats made against them, there are kidnappings here and all over Mexico. We don't want people to know our names."

"Then I won't use your names," I said.

A small crowd had gathered in the lobby by now, about a half dozen of the sixty or so people who belong to the congregation. Some of them spoke among themselves, a few of them drifted over to our discussion.

"We'll ask the rabbi," a woman said.

"I'll tell the rabbi what the board decided," Mrs. S. said.

"But now it's time for the service," the other woman said.

"Are you coming in?" Mrs. S. said, half inquiring, half inviting.

"Not under your conditions," I said. "If I come in, I'll be keeping my eyes open. You've just told me that I'm not welcome to write my story. So I'm not welcome."

"No, you can't write your story," Mrs. S. said.

"Then I can't come in," I said.

A third congregant who had been listening to us edged over to me, a slightly built, dark-haired middle-aged woman who spoke with a French accent.

"You must come in," she said. "You are a Jew, yes?"

I thought a moment. Then I nodded, yes.

"You are invited then, story or no story," the woman with the French accent said. "And besides, there is such a thing as free speech which I am afraid this person doesn't understand." She glanced over at Mrs. S., and rolled her eyes.

"*You* don't understand," Mrs. S. said to her. "Some of us are rich. We've gotten death threats, there have been kidnappings. We don't want our names in the newspaper. You don't have money, you don't understand."

The French woman's head jerked back as though she'd been struck on the jaw.

"Oh," she said, "you know nothing about me. Nothing at all." She turned away from Mrs. S. and pleaded with me to come into the synagogue.

But I could not enter their sanctuary, knowing that I was going in not only as a Jew and a guest but also to gather impressions for this story. The French woman said that they would speak to the rabbi about this matter. I told them that I would wait to hear his decision.

While waiting in the vestibule I mulled over the many ironies of the situation, for me and for these people. While I had nodded in assent to the woman's question about whether or not I was Jewish, I had in my own mind many questions about this question.

I had been born into a Jewish family, yes, and circumcised in the first few days of life. I had attended religious school, though my parents never did more than practice the minimum amounts of Jewish ritual, my mother lighting candles on the eve of the Sabbath, my father attending the services at the Orthodox synagogue only on the High Holy Days in the autumn of the year. I practiced for my bar mitzvah, the male coming-of-age ceremony celebrated when a boy turns thirteen. But after high school I had fallen away from the religion. In the past forty years I had been to synagogue once, and that, ironically enough, had been in 1976 in Mexico City where I had attended a Saturday morning service in a small synagogue near a freight crossing in a workers' district in the north part of town, a small, plaster-walled structure with poor lighting and meager accoutrements. This was the place of prayer for the self-proclaimed "nucleus of Mexican Jewry," a small group of men and boys, women and noisy, rollicking children, presided over by the aging Rabbi Baltazar Laureano Ramírez, all of them mestizos who claimed to be descended from the first Jews to set foot on Mexican soil, Jews like those in the family of Hernando Alonso.

So if I had paid only one visit to a synagogue in forty years, at least it had been an interesting place!

The only other official ceremony I had attended was the burial service for my father at his graveside some fourteen years ago. And I had raised none of my children as Jews; certainly none of them had a Jewish mother. But the Ashkenazi tribe and its culture was my birthright, and I had been more than mildly interested in the debates going on in Israel about the nature of Jewish identity. Who was a Jew? The strict Orthodox rabbis of Israel, who presided over the country's official religion with no less iron in their hands than the ayatollahs of Iran, made it clear that they would not recognize marriages of Jews by blood to converts to Conservative or Reform Judaism.

And over the course of this very week, speaking to various rabbis and Jewish lay people here and in San Diego, the question of the religious identity of converts to Judaism stayed with me. A name kept coming up, the name of a man in Tijuana, Carlos Salas, who was supposedly a Conservative rabbi or cantor who was converting Tijuana Catholics to Judaism. An Orthodox rabbi from the San Diego Chabad movement, Rabbi Michael Lieder, dismissed the possibility that anyone who wasn't converted by

Orthodox procedures was a real Jew. To him, and the rest of the Chabad members, there are two kinds of Jews, those who were Jews by birth and those who are converted by the Orthodox means. By that standard, I was who I was. But is an observant Jewish convert to Conservative Judaism less a Jew than I am? According to the recent radical declaration of the fundamentalist Union of Orthodox Rabbis of the United States and Canada, Conservative and Reform Judaism are "a different religion," and therefore any convert to those branches of the faith are not, in the eyes of these fundamentalists, Jews at all.

A few small children, the hope of the congregation, ran through the vestibule and out into the courtyard where the sanctuary stood, crossing a line that my ethics would not allow me to pass over. I recalled the many hours I had spent as a child, playing out the long boredom outside the synagogue on the High Holy Days while the adults within prayed themselves into a sort of chanting, humming, buzzing, mumbling mass of supplicants to a stern, demanding God who had first appeared to the earliest Jew hidden within a burning bush and asked a father to sacrifice his son to his worship. The first rabbi I recall meeting was a sour-breathed man with five o'clock shadow, a real Old World Orthodox trooper whose way of greeting young boys was to take a fold of your cheek between his fingers and pull hard.

"You're a good boy? You better stay good!"

Feeling the pinch and breathing in his breath, who couldn't wait to get away?

The cantor was a huskier man, and sweeter, with a rich baritone voice that swelled the upper reaches of the synagogue on the High Holy Days nearly to bursting with the beauty of his noise and with its more subtle minor meanderings in lesser keys called to mind the ancient days of the desert tribe that first invented the figure of a single, all-powerful deity who kept to himself and demanded complete fealty to his every commandment. Between the fear of getting pinched and the pleasure of such music, a small boy could live in the faith of his fathers. It was a good time, life in the cocoon of family and tribe and neighborhood and welcoming Jersey shore town, though it lasted only a few comforting years before I crossed over the border into the disquiet of uncertainty. Who am I? And what am I? And who are my people? A tribe or a group of co-religionists? What makes a Jew? His mother's blood? Or his religious practice? And if the latter, then why care about such antique and vexing questions as the nature of bloodlines and the purity of the tribe? Figure and ground, the questions and the answers dart back and forth. The People of the Book? The Jews have always been People on the Border, standing at the interface between past and present, ancient and modern, Old World and New World, between blood tribe and practitioners of a faith. And why do I feel the need for them to care about me? And why do I care about them?

The Centro's long-time janitor, a mestizo man, lounged in a soft chair at one corner of the hall, his white skullcap perched precariously on his head. Another employee of the Centro paced in and out of the hall, his small ponytail dangling behind him. A third man stood outside, watching the parked cars. There had been some vandalism awhile ago, he told me. And so he worked security. And I wondered if a Mexican Jew could ever walk outside to see his vehicle vandalized and write it off as nothing but a crime instead of as a crime against a Jew?

I look out along the corridor to the sanctuary and see that some people are coming out of the service. A man my age appears with the two young men I had spoken to upon my arrival. He is their father, younger than I am but to my eyes he has the appearance of a much older man, and he reminds me of my own father. We speak a little about his line of work. He sells perfumes. A good business. One of his sons has gone into public relations, the other still studying at college on the other side of the border but also helping out with the family business. I know these people. I feel at home with them. We are related by culture, though they are Sephardim of Turkish origins originally. Perhaps we'll speak further if I am allowed to stay for the community dinner.

But Mrs. S. comes out of the sanctuary to inform me that she has spoken to the rabbi and he has said that because it is the Sabbath he doesn't want to engage in this discussion. So the decision of the board still stands. No story. They won't cooperate. On Wednesday, she tells me, they will meet again and discuss the situation. They will send me guidelines. Where can they fax them to me? So she has bent a little to some pressure from the others. But not enough to invite me in to the meal.

I leave the building, a Jew—?—turned away by his own—?— people.

8—*Another Sanctuary*

But in Tijuana there is another sanctuary for Jews, if they will only open their eyes to see it. In the Montebello neighborhood, halfway up a hill in the southeastern section of the city, at Calle Amado Nervo No. 207, you approach the outside wall of a small compound and if you raise your eyes you discover, of all remarkable things in this working class Catholic neighborhood, a large menorah, the candelabra that is the symbol of the Jewish holiday of Chanukah. This is the sign upon the door that leads into the Congregación Hebrea de Baja California, a Conservative-oriented Temple presided over by Maestro Carlos Salas Díaz.

As you enter the compound, to the right you see new construction, to the left the entryway, a quiet space with muted light that leads to the archway that opens onto the sanctuary. Soft blue tiles made by Jewish artisans in Valencia line the walls and give back a gentle effusion of color. There are seats for about seventy-five people facing the traditional closed Ark of the Covenant in which rest two Torahs, one of them a gift from a community of Russian immigrants from Los Angeles.

Presiding over this sanctuary is a big broad-faced bear of a man in his mid-sixties, clearly mestizo in appearance, who possesses an attractive mixture of humility and charisma. In another life Carlos Salas might have been an upper echelon official of the PRI or a successful lawyer. From a pamphlet that he has had printed based on a 1995 San Diego Tribune feature story by Arthur Golden, the unusual life-journey of this unusual man unfolds like a modern-day fable. Born in the mountains of the central Mexican state of Zacatecas, one of eight children of Catholic parents, Salas knew a childhood full of relative calm. His father was a miner who worked in the gold and silver mines in nearby Fresnillo. Starting at the age of five, young Carlos worked as a shepherd until he entered public school four years later. One of his older brothers eventually emigrated to the United States and Salas, when he turned eighteen, followed him to Buffalo, New York, and found work as an apprentice mechanic for Bethlehem Steel. He remained employed there until he was drafted into the U.S. Army.

Picture the young Zacatecan in Alaska where he served most of his tour of duty! The cold, the whiteness became a great blank screen that allowed him to turn his inquiring Mexican immigrant's mind inward! To thoughts about the nature of spirit and mortality!

But when he returned to Buffalo, the army veteran still had a head full of the workaday world. He used his savings to buy a small hotel and married his first wife, Ariela Valdivia, a Cuban American woman, with whom he had five children. His spiritual quest led him to enter the Methodist Institute of Buffalo, a now-defunct seminary, and he became an ordained minister, preaching at several Buffalo area churches with Spanish-speaking congregations. Then, moved by the desire for a warmer climate, he moved to Los Angeles.

For the next decade Salas seemed to travel along two roads simultaneously, finding success in business even as he followed his spiritual bent. His boyhood ties to gold and silver pointed him toward the jewelry business. His love of scripture and writing in general led to work as a reporter for a local Spanish-language newspaper. His instincts for organization gave him the idea for another successful venture, a secretarial and translation service in the same building as the Mexican consulate in downtown Los Angeles.

Salas's investments made him rich enough to take the time to satisfy his hunger for news about the Old Testament and its laws that his Methodist training could not satisfy. In 1962, Salas enrolled in a five-year course of study at the University of Judaism in Bel Air, the West Coast branch of the Jewish Theological Seminary. The closer he came to renouncing his Methodist beliefs and embracing Judaism as a religion the more avuncular his teachers became.

"You're crazy," Rabbi Henry Fisher told Salas.

"You're going to have nothing but heartache," another rabbi told him as Salas plunged into a second round of study. Then came his official conversion in 1967.

Jews have never been big on converting people from another religion to Judaism, at least not since the end of that turbulent period, dubbed by one classical scholar as "The Age of Anxiety," that extended from the first century BC to the end of the first century after the birth of Christ. Numerous religions, most with a compelling message, vied in those years of spiritual frenzy and misdirection, for the souls of the population of the Mediterranean. Worship Astarte, or Cybele, or Jesus, or the God of Abraham, or join the ranks of the bull-worshippers from the Roman army—these were some of the choices people saw before them. And as far as proselytizing went, the Jews did not do badly, taking numbers of souls where they found them among the questing and tormented citizens of Rome and its extremities. With a thousand years of commentaries on the Old Testament, and all of its concomitant laws, still lying ahead of it, Judaism was not a terribly difficult religion to master, except for the painful requirement of male circumcision. But it was still less strenuous a choice than bull-worship, which required, among other things, a trek through the Italian outback and a bath in the blood of a full-grown bull. However when Christianity, with its simple demand of a decision to worship Jesus as a personal savior, began to get the upper hand, Jewish proselytizing fell off. And never became a paramount concern for Jews thereafter. Then came the Inquisition when conversions went the other way and thousands of Spanish Jews took instruction in Christianity and raised their children in the church, thinking, mistakenly as it turned out, that this would give them and their descendants shelter in a murderous time.

So conversion is not a subject that Jews think about very often, and when they do it is not usually in a positive way. Because of the large percentage of American Jews who marry outside the religion, conversion has become a topic of interest in the United States. Some spouses choose to study to become Jews. But the numbers are not large. Of the five and a half million Jews in the United States, only 185,000 are converts. Most of these are Conservative converts, at home in the United States but in Israel found by the Israeli Orthodox rabbis to be counterfeit Jews.

But whatever the Orthodox of Israel—and that fundamentalist group of American and Canadian Orthodox rabbis—may say, the conversion process remains quite rigorous. Normally a board of three Conservative rabbis sits in judgment on someone who has announced his or her intention to convert to Judaism, asking questions about their knowledge of Judaism and their motivations for converting to the religion. A successful session is followed by an immersion ceremony, in which the newly embraced converts are led into the mikva, the ritual bath. In the case of Carlos Salas, *seven* rabbis gathered on the tribunal, evidence that the word had gotten around the Bel Air seminary that an extraordinary event was about to take place. And if some possibly had come to scoff, most stayed to praise.

Salas had scarcely dried off from his ritual immersion when he left Los Angeles for Mexico. He already owned a house and some property in Tijuana, a location that he saw as a place of promise for business and at the same time a city where many of the inhabitants suffered greatly and were in need of spiritual counseling. Or as he described it to me one recent Sabbath afternoon, a city with people "wandering in the streets, looking to the left, looking to the right, and seeing nothing." Salas opened a school where he offered free Bible study classes and the classes quickly filled up with interested, inquiring local people, most of them from the ranks of the ordinary workforce of the town, a few of them from the professions. And like his father before him, he became a sort of miner, his bank account filling up because of an innovative procedure that he developed for salvaging gold tailings from the residue of jewelry workshop dust. He also married again, to Cristina, a now forty-year-old lawyer with the Mexican Social Security Institute, with whom he has had four children, a son and three daughters.

Elias, his son, is a slender, quiet young man, dressed neatly and with a good handshake. On the afternoon that I met him, he had a young boy in tow, and a mission in mind. The child was a fatherless boy from the neighborhood whom the Salas family is caring for. Elias was taking him to the circus. By the standards of any Orthodox rabbi, whether from the fundamentalists or the mainstream or the Chabad "God Squad," this certainly wouldn't be classified as good Jewish practice. But when you consider just where any million Jews you might follow on a Sabbath afternoon could be heading, it doesn't seem contrary to the unwritten laws for the care and upbringing of a fatherless young boy.

Many of Maestro Salas's students in the Bible study classes began to follow along the path that he had first taken, away from Catholicism and toward Judaism, not so much out of rejection of the former faith as a way of getting closer to its origins. In 1984, nearly two dozen people expressed the desire to leap ahead rather than merely walk. And so Maestro Salas led the first handful of Tijuana residents desiring to convert to Judaism up to Los Angeles where they sat before a rabbinical tribunal at the University of Judaism. As Arthur Golden has reported, the chairman of conversion affairs for the western region of the (Conservative) rabbinical assembly, Rabbi Edward M. Tenenbaum, said of the applicants that they "were reasonably well-prepared." Rabbi Tenenbaum went on to say, "You don't expect a convert to know everything about Judaism. What stood out was Salas's devotion to the converts and their devotion to him..." In a dramatic gesture, the group drove to Rosarito Beach and took their required ritual bath by wading into the ocean. Two more groups of converts have gone forward since then, one in 1991, comprised of twenty-nine people, again at the University of Judaism, and in January of 1995, another class of thirty-four people.

Since he wasn't born Jewish, Maestro Salas grew up without
what seems to be the often endemic paranoia of the modern Jew
in the wake of the Holocaust. He has good relations with the
Catholic Church in Tijuana and has converted his neighbors,
without them even knowing it, into a group of philosemites. When
they hear that a visiting congregation from Southern California is
driving down for a tour of the Congregación Hebrea compound,
they sweep the sidewalks and the streets and cheer the visitors
when they arrive. Much of this has to do with the way that Salas
has reached out to the local inhabitants with gifts of food and cash
to the needy. Currently under construction in his compound is a
dining hall in which he plans to feed free breakfast to the hungry
every morning of the year.

But if his relations with the Church and his Catholic neighbors
are good, his ties to the Centro Israelita couldn't be worse. At best,
people speak of him as "the preacher turned rabbi." Others prefer
not to talk about him at all, or they dismiss his group as a cult.
But there is an even more negative way of describing him. "It's a
touchy subject," one prominent Jewish businessman told me. "He's
doing a good job. But they're not Jewish over there."

Not Jewish! Think how the Nazis studied the genealogy of
populations in Germany and France in hopes of discovering some
drop of Jewish blood! To be declared not Jewish was a sentence
of life! Though Jewish law forbids disenfranchisement of other
Jews, today the Orthodox wade through a crowd of people who
believe they are Jews, winnowing out those whom they deem to
have failed to meet the test of practice, symbolically killing off
those whom they find to be less than observant. Obey only four
hundred of the five hundred and some laws of the *halachah*, the
compendium of Jewish theological practice over the centuries, and
they will consider you less than what you may take yourself to be.

Is this merely a version of High Church snobbism? Or is there something in it in the Orthodox view that harks back to the earliest days of this desert-born tribal religion when the Hebrews found themselves singled out by a jealous God as His agent in history, showing the way to the nations of idol worshippers and unbelievers? Add the elements of racial difference to the mix and you come up with quite a complicated situation. Is Maestro Salas a Jew? Are his children, raised in a home attentive to Jewish custom and law, Jewish?

It was one thing when some years ago he was rebuffed by the board when asked if he could participate in the activities of the Centro. His children learned an even harder lesson when they went there to study in one of the Bible classes and Mrs. S. asked them to leave. They did not belong, she told them. They have not been back, and it may be that this particular act of rudeness on the part of Mrs. S. may have sundered relations between the two groups for good and all. With its undertones of racism—denying entry to the Jewish children of Mexican birth, in fact, denying the possibility that these Mexican children might be Jewish at all—the autocratic action of the woman now co-head of Tijuana's Orthodox community makes it appear that she believes that the dark-skinned Mexican Jews, those who resemble in appearance the janitors and security guards at the Centro rather than most of the congregants, are theologically, socially, and racially inferior. And if the children of Hernando Alonso knocked at the door of the Centro, would they, too, be turned away?

9—Meditations on a Myth

The story of the death by fire of Hernando Alonso is a powerful thing to consider. The Jew in flames! With those bonfires fed

by Jewish fuel, the great golden age of triadic Spanish culture—
Catholic, Jewish, Muslim—came to an end. And you can say that
such a run of destruction as the Inquisition presaged the destruction
of European Jewry by the Nazis in the twentieth century, or you can
just notice the similarities. After a great period of peace and inter-
communal beneficence, an age of great art and music and literature,
the nation, like some magnificent edifice built on unsteady soil,
came crashing down into a boiling pit of race hate and murder.

Could it happen again in Mexico? More pyres? More Jews thrown
into the flames? There are some who fear the worst. There are some
who, pondering the current high profile of Jew-hating militias and
so-called Christian Identity churches that preach a doctrine of
racial "purity," say that it could happen in the United States, the
stereotype of the high-minded dark-robed Spanish Inquisitor or the
neatly tailored Gestapo officer, his nails well manicured, turning off
the Beethoven on the victrola to settle down to serious questioning
of his Jewish captive, replaced by the image of a lanky, long-jawed
Yank in camouflage clothes, squatting over a latrine hole, his drawers
down about his ankles, an unfiltered cigarette dangling from his
narrow lips, defecating on the Jew in the pit.

Disgusting! The nightmares, I say, of a neurotic-depressive
imagination, and not a useful thought to consider when meditating
on the millennial prospects of the Jewish immigrant. There is, in
fact, a much more evocative New World story to consider, an ur-
story, a myth, we have to call it, that has persisted for centuries
that puts the Jew as the *first* to arrive on New World soil. In North
America, for example, in the theology of the Mormon Church,
the story persists that the Lost Tribe of Israel emigrated by ship
from the Middle East to the American continent. Some early U.S.
chroniclers of the mores of the North American Plains Indians
wrote of the amazing similarities between the rituals of certain

tribes and Jewish ritual. Anthropologists dig all over Mexico even as you read this, some of their work sponsored by the Mormons, inspired by this old story of the tie between the Biblical lands and the territory of the New World, the myth that the Lost Tribe of Israel sailed from the Holy Land to Mexico, carrying with them the ancient scrolls of the Law, in the same way that Aeneas in Virgil's great poem of the founding of Rome carried the hearth gods from the city of Troy to the shores of Italy.

Certainly a number of legitimate anthropologists and researchers have based their work on the possibility of such a voyage. Thor Heyerdahl made his famous raft "Kon-Tiki" to show that a reed boat could survive such a trip. Ivan Van Sertima, a Rutgers University scholar, has written extensively on the ocean-going traffic between Africa, the Near East, and the Mexican coast where the mysterious Olmecs thrived and left behind the huge stone heads with inexplicably African features. And if we can skate for an instant to the furthest rim of the links between mythology and history, consider the story of Quetzalcoatl, the Plumed Serpent, God of the Aztecs, whom theology proclaimed would arrive in the flesh from over the great waters to the East and bring to a conclusion one of the great cycles of time. As the Spanish chroniclers of the period suggest, the Aztecs mistook Cortés for Quetzalcoatl. But what if the Plumed Serpent had already arrived and the working out of the myth in the time of the Conquistadors was a faint replay of an early Advent on American soil? What if the Plumed Serpent, Quetzalcoatl Himself, had been a Jew?

All these speculations, fantasies, myths, and dreams! a far cry you may say from the life of the Jews of contemporary Mexico, with their ties to Europe, either Spain or Germany, Poland, and Russia. And yet there are those Mexican Jews—people who call themselves Jews, as the Orthodox would say—who claim an inheritance that goes far enough back in time to link them to the period of the Conquest, people who claim that their ancestors miraculously survived the period of the Mexican Inquisition and passed along their rituals from generation to generation, these indigenous people, native in appearance, who read and write Hebrew, and participate in all of the rituals of the faith some of whom I met myself that Sabbath morning in 1976 in the synagogue on Calle Caruso in Mexico City. In the agricultural village of Venta Prieta, in fact, there are a thousand such families who make these claims, people whose ancestors apparently went underground during the Mexican Inquisition instead of fleeing north across the border to territory that we now call the state of New Mexico, families whose grave markers display small Stars of David along with the crosses and whose lives are filled with the rituals—blessings of bread and wine, observance of the Sabbath, sacramental marriage—that have bound Jews together as co-religionists over millennia.

The story that the Lost Tribe of Israel sailed to Mexico may remain always a myth. But it opens a door onto fabulous thoughts of historical continuity and raises provocative questions about the nature of religious identity. The Indian Jews I met, and those thousands more gathered in the village of Venta Prieta, may be the apparent descendants of the Mexican Judaizers long lost to the flames of the Inquisition, the children of Hernando Alonso, and a kind of Lost Tribe themselves, whose time may possibly have come around again.

10—*Jews at the Door*

On Sunday, March 16, Maestro Carlos Salas flew to Mexico City where he met with representatives from the Jews of Venta Prieta in preparation for a trip to their village. Ignored for decades by the Jewish community of Mexico City, the Venta Prieta residents apparently wish to affiliate themselves with a central religious organization and it seems as though the Congregación Hebrea de Baja California may be the place where they will join.

Carlos Salas already has plans to expand his Tijuana compound to accommodate a large influx of these new congregants from the east of Mexico. And what a day that will be when they arrive! A great day for these descendants of Hernando Alonso and a great day for the city of Tijuana as well! Rather ironically, it seems as though just at the time that the Centro of the Orthodox Jews, those bound to the religion by blood, is rapidly disintegrating, and the worldwide debate on the nature of Jewish identity rising to a crescendo, convert Maestro Salas is building a peaceful new little Jerusalem on a hill on the east side of this frenetic border town and opening his doors to all who would enter.

Originally published in the San Diego Reader

THE WATERY
PART OF
THE WORLD

A TRANCE AFTER BREAKFAST

A little after 9:00 on a beautiful August morning, after our breakfast of fresh papaya and astringent lemon-ginger tea on a nearby hotel balcony, a man just about ten feet in front of me—one of eight men in a long row—took a dagger by the hilt with both hands and plunged it into his chest just above his heart.

Except the point didn't puncture his flesh.

He tried and tried, worked it and worked it, while I sat squirming, I have to say, nearly writhing in my front-row seat at the small outdoor pavilion. A gamelan orchestra, all sixteen players, made their otherworldly music, a skein of pongs and chongs they beat out with fancy hammers on their marimba-like instruments, with a few flutes accompanying and a master gong that set the major intervals with austere, reverberating bongs (which taken together sound something like the Lionel Hampton Orchestra on LSD) while the front line of kris dancers, as they're called after the name of their daggers, the kris knife, kept on trying to penetrate their chests—to no avail. These men, Hindu priests, bare-chested, barefooted, and wearing the ubiquitous sarong, were lost in a trance, an altered state induced by a series of prayers and offerings to the gods.

And so, in my own way, was I.

The dancers had emerged onto the stone stage in the village of Batubulan, a fifteen minute drive or so from our hotel in the central Balinese town of Ubud—which some wag, before I arrived here on this astonishing little island, had described to me, because of all of its artisans, as the Santa Fe of Bali—at the climax of the Barong Dance, one of the several so-called trance dances that make up the core of the Balinese religious theatrical repertoire. For me, it seemed like the climax of a long and hypnotic journey across the island that had begun long before we had actually set foot in the place.

Bali, Bali, Bali, the name had bonged and chimed in many a conversation between me and my wife, a choreographer, dancer, and massage therapist who, though a stark and wonderful creator of modern dance, had as an undergraduate dance student at an arts college in Missouri donned a sari and felt as though she should have been born in one. (She had studied Indian dance forms with a teacher in Massachusetts and taught for ten years at the London School of Contemporary Dance. And read and read about Asian dance and seen it performed over the years by visiting companies, but had never witnessed it live in its local habitation.) Bali, Bali, Bali, that was where she wanted to visit, and so, in the summer of our tenth wedding anniversary (perhaps, I can call it now, with some hindsight, the last summer of twenty-first-century American innocence) she signed up for a small group tour of the island, a "healing arts tour," that would include visits to local medicine men, temple ceremonies, ceremonial dances, and also daily yoga practice, with me, group skeptic, just tagging along.

Like most people, I had been to numerous religious ceremonies in my lifetime and, like many others, had seen my share of dance performances, both classical and modern. And I had traveled a bit around the world. But no amount of years as a child in a synagogue or as an adult on the occasions of weddings and funerals and holidays in churches of various denominations—Catholic and Protestant, Buddhist and Shinto—had prepared me for Bali. At first breath, I knew I had arrived in a special place.

The freshly narcotic air outside our hotel porch embossed with the perfume of frangipani blossoms and tuberoses; the old temple wall we walked along just as soon as we arrived at the airport at the capital, Denpesar; the huge statue at the traffic rotary at the airport exit commemorating a battle from the great Hindu epic the Ramayana; the small temples within the family compounds that we passed on a drive from the beach up into the mountains of North Bali; the skirts of checkered material—black and white for yin and yang, good and evil—and the offerings, the ubiquitous offerings of flowers and incense in every doorway, on every set of steps, in the ledges of the stone shrines that lined the roadways more numerous by hundreds than post boxes along an American street: the little altars everywhere proclaimed that people here, at worst, elevated what we Westerners normally take to be mere superstition to everyday reality and, at best, gave it a good name.

From our first hour onward, I went along with it, thinking that I was merely behaving politely, a good trooper. Upon our arrival on a misty afternoon in Munduk, a small mountain village amid clove and coffee and banana plantations and rice paddies, we immediately received a lesson in the construction of these offerings from the sandalwood-hued woman in white blouse and sarong who attended to them for all of the cottages on the property where we were staying. Our model was the small, ashtray-size palm-leaf box that holds another small leaf cut in the manner of origami and a number of small flowers, with a thumb-sized blossom called the pandan at the heart of the arrangement, this presided over by a smoking stick of incense.

I threw myself into the work and, in my own clumsy way, put one of these together, as did my wife, and we offered them to the local gods on the balcony of our little rice-barn-shaped cottage. And didn't it work! How else to explain what we see before us when the mountain mist lifted, the incredible multitiered beauty, layer upon layer of light of varying intensity, rice paddies in the foreground, with the constant musical accompaniment of the water running in the irrigation ditches that served them, leading our eyes across a series of palm-fringed ridges that descended all the way to the distant glistening plain of the Java Sea. Dozens of swifts dipped and swerved above the rice fields on the shimmering air of late afternoon, tallying up their daily fill of insects. Offstage, cocks crowed and motorbikes, Bali's main mode of transportation, sputtered and growled like small dogs meeting at a crossroads.

Our days in the island's high altitudes consisted of treks through the countryside that, on first, and second, and even third look, resembled something like Eden's own horticulture. Multiple varieties of bananas, and papaya growing everywhere, and other fruit both familiar and unfamiliar, and flowers and spices—jack fruit and mangosteen and avocado, monkey fruit, the infamous foul-smelling (and delicious) durian, snake skin fruit and monkey tail, hibiscus flowers and wild poinsettia, taro and cassava and coffee and cacao and ginger, betel nut, arica nut, lemon grass, lemon basil, and nutmeg. Rice paddies rose in terraced layers up every incline, like green wedding cakes waiting to be sliced. Along the narrow roads, spices lay splashed across long mats or on brushed earth, drying in the sun, so that the air tasted everywhere of coffee and cloves.

Our nights up here saw us tottering on the edge of early bedtimes, giving ourselves up to the romantic intensity of celebrating our anniversary in these surroundings, making much of it, and then falling into the deepest sleep beneath mosquito netting that made us feel as though we were on safari and under the signal care of the tribes of gecko lizards that walked upside down on our cottage ceiling, chirping every now and then as if ordering spiders from some recalcitrant waiter invisible in the dark.

Before too many nights passed, my soul settled down, like a feather floating toward earth in a windless sky.

I'd awake before it was light, sit up in bed and do a twenty-minute meditation and then dress and sit out on the balcony in the coolness of the pre-dawn air, listening to the earliest birds and insects warming up for their sunrise performances. Equipped with penlight and book lamp, I'd read and make notes, make notes and read. After a while the dark began to drain away like water from a leaking pool, and there it was again—not a hallucination but a view with the same intensity as dream—the rice paddies, the tiers of hills, the Java Sea some thirty miles away as the bird flies, at this early hour just catching the first notice that the sun was rising on the other side of the island.

If making love had seemed like the perfect act as the night began, a yoga session on the open-air pavilion seemed right for early morning. Flowing from one pose to another, under the tutelage of the gentle-voiced instructor traveling with us, it felt as though our shifts and reanglings of muscle and bone were somehow tuned to the transitions of light and shade as the first full light of the new sun touched a match to the surface of the ocean. While we moved, a priest all in white, loaned to the guest houses

from the village, walked silently on bare feet to the shrine at the
edge of our pavilion to lay smoking sticks of incense across flower
offerings at the base and on the top. Another day, another attempt
to ward off low-level spirits of nuisance and harm.

"Going native" is what the old nineteenth-century British
imperial keepers of the flame used to call giving oneself over to
the local traditions and it was considered a bit of a disgrace to
be caught out in it. But if one of the most sophisticated and at
the same time simplest arguments on behalf of Christianity is the
seventeenth-century French philosopher Blaise Pascal's so-called
wager—that if you believe in God you gain if there is a God and
if there isn't you have lost nothing for the effort—then it couldn't
hurt a rather skeptical American writer to return to his cottage
each morning after yoga and light a stick of incense as part of his
own daily offering.

A week later it certainly seemed like the right thing to do to
put on a sarong and temple sash—garments you must wear to gain
entry into most of the thousands of temples on the island—and
take a bracing dip in the purifying waters of the sacred springs at
the Tempaksiring temple outside Ubud. On another brilliant sunlit
August morning, hundreds of Hindu pilgrims had come to pray
and bathe, but there was no great rush at the pools themselves,
where the natural springs gushed out of nine demon-faced spigots,
seven of those reserved for the living, two of them set aside for the
purification of the dead.

Barefoot, and feeling somewhat awkward and constricted in the
tight-fitting sarong, I eased myself into the cold spring pool, the
water coming up to my chest. I trod lightly over the stony bottom,
holy carp and gold fish scurrying at my approach, pushing aside
the flotsam of blossoms and twigs of expired incense, making my
way to the first spigot, bowing my head and making the mudra of

completion with my fingers and hands that I had learned to use at the end of every yoga session, as the ice-sharp water spilled over my skull.

If it had only just been my head! I never imagined—why should I have?—just how cold life could be beneath a sarong, feeling the liquid swirl around my thighs and genitals, and worrying about how vulnerable I was as the edge of my garment swirled up around my hips to nibbles from hungry fish and the fate that awaited me if I did not make enough obeisance to the local powers and those beyond. I moved from spigot to spigot, splashed and bathed, bowed my head and raised my face to the chilly flow, asking the gods of the place to ward off evil spirits great and small, to abate the nastiness of rumor, the jealousy of enemies, and give me the wisdom to see my life as it needed to be lived, free of dread and angst, and feeling whatever power I might possess radiating from head to toe, from fingertip to fingertip, brain to heart to liver and knees and guts.

That night we witnessed our first trance dance, the ancient Kecak or Monkey Chant. A hundred men, young to old, bare-chested and wearing stripped-down sarongs, gathered around a bonfire with arms across each other's shoulders to perform a chant as hypnotic in its own way as Gregorian song but in its rhythmical complexity sounding so much older and essential as to make plainsong seem only half the music it aspired to be and as bland as a Pat Boone ballad. And the monkey chanters were followed by a wiry old fellow from the Ubud community whose eyes gazed way past the edge of the audience toward some point on the horizon of infinity as he rode a wooden horse into a blazing bonfire—he himself being "ridden" by one of the local gods, is how the Balinese describe such trances—kicking at the fire, dancing on it, bathing in it, drinking the sparks.

Those sparks still sputtered in my mind when the next morning after breakfast we drove to Batubulan to see the Barong Dance with its kris knife finale. And though it wasn't the finale of our stay on this marvelous island, it marked the time for me when I had to admit just how much I had given in to the spirit of the place. Walking backstage with our guide, I had the opportunity to pick up one of the knives the priests had used in the dance, feeling the substantial heft of it and gingerly touching the sharp point to my own chest.

"Some of the dancers do fake it," our travel leader said, himself a dancer and the son of a priest, "and some have died trying it. And some are exactly what you see."

I was mulling this over—mull, mull, mull, the whirring of what the Buddhists call the reckless monkey mind—at the beginning of another trek a few days later. After a rich morning filled with many marvelous encounters with the sort of gifted local artisans that Bali produces as naturally as cloves and coffee beans, and after a drive to East Bali for a delicious lunch of crab cakes and papaya juice beneath a breezy pavilion at the edge of the Indian Ocean, we drove away from the beaches, taking the narrow roads up into the mountains again, on a little pilgrimage to the so-called Mother Temple at Besakih, midway up the slope leading to Mt. Agung, the island's most active volcano and one of its most sacred places.

With the upper part of Agung veiled in fast-moving clouds I could only guess at the mountain's true height. But geography wasn't foremost on my mind as once again in sarongs and sashes we walked among a thousand Balinese worshippers, and then sat with them on the hard temple stones, listening to the white-garbed priests chanting prayers in Cawi, the old Javanese tongue, listening to the tinkling of the small bells handled by the priests, breathing in the mix of mountain air and incense, and putting forward our own offerings—the palm leaf holding flowers, the incense burning. A priest walked slowly up and down the many rows of seated devotees sprinkling holy water and casting blessings.

At last he reached us! A few drops touched my head! And for a moment I understood why we had traveled ten thousand miles to visit this particular place. Turning to catch a glimpse of the fading tapestry of late afternoon light, I saw rice fields, palm plantations, and only an hour or so drive down the winding roads some of the most beautiful beaches on earth where thousands of Japanese and Australian and European and American tourists sunbathed and sipped fruit drinks and beer and champagne while the tropical ocean beckoned beyond them. And then I turned back to gaze up at the sacred volcano as the wind tore the clouds aside to reveal the physical beauty—and hint at the deeper mystery—of the peak which had been there, though hidden from us, all along.

Originally published in Gourmet

KIWI DREAMS

There's a traffic jam on the road to Paradise, a three-car lockup along this pitted, gravel track about five miles north of the hamlet of Glenorchy, at the western end of Lake Wakatipu—how remote is this!—the largest inland body of water in all of New Zealand, South Island or North.

Here where the ozone layer has thinned out nearly to nothing, the sun is glowing brilliantly and the sky is a lovely translucent off-blue, and I'm sitting in my rental car with the windows rolled down, enjoying an antipodean seventy-degree January afternoon. Two other cars (three cars constituting a traffic jam in this near-wilderness area of this sparsely populated twin-island nation in the South Pacific) have stopped just ahead of me, their drivers considering the wisdom, as I will be in a moment, of driving down into and across a six-foot-wide culvert filled with rushing water and rocks.

The first car begins rolling slowly forward, dips down into the culvert, bobs along like a cork on the ocean, and makes its way up the other side. The second car suddenly follows. I glance around at the inquisitive cows that have wandered close to the road to observe us, and then drive forward myself, saying a prayer for the rental company's axles and then bouncing down and up, gazing out at the dust cloud stirred by the first two cars as I catch sight of my goal, a line of beech trees about a half mile ahead, silvery green against the backdrop of azure river and snowcapped mountain peaks.

What am I doing here? I ask myself as a caravan of four-wheel drive vehicles with the logo Nomad Tours on their doors comes barreling along in a cloud of dust from the opposite direction, taking the culvert with the ease of kids playing hopscotch.

Blame it on the movies. As one Hollywood reporter recently wrote, in the category of Academy Awards for Best Locations, New Zealand would win hands down. Here at the edge of Mt. Aspiring National Park, on the border of a private estate named after the mythical part of the heavens from which John Milton has the angel Satan fall, director Peter Jackson filmed the dreamy Lothlorien episodes of *The Lord of the Rings* trilogy. The drivers and passengers in those other cars and in those four-wheel drive Nomads have probably read about this in an article in the in-flight magazine of Air New Zealand, or discovered this fact, as I did, in Ian Brodie's *The Lord of the Rings Location Guidebook*, one hundred and twenty-eight pages of lore that covers just about every location in the film trilogy. So all of us out here, we're rubber-necking at a place that exists only in a movie.

It goes even deeper than that. While watching *The Lord of the Rings* led me on this mini-quest up the Paradise road, I had many other New Zealand movie images in my mind as I sat awake during the twelve-hour night flight over the Pacific from Los Angeles to Auckland—among them, the dark beach with the abandoned piano and the furious surf in Jane Campion's lyrical 1993 movie

The Piano. My immediate goal upon arriving in Auckland was to find that beach which, I had learned, was as the crow flies only about fifteen miles west of the center of the city, on the shore of the Tasman Sea.

But as I drove myself and my wife west out of the country's largest city in a heavy early morning storm—summer rain in our part of the world was never like this, so hard and so constant—crossing bridges and viaducts to pass over the water that makes up so much of Auckland's domain, the weather proved too difficult and our map too vague, so we decided to turn north toward our destination for the night, the tiny town of Russell on the northeast coast of the North Island and save the beach for later in our stay.

By mid-morning the skies began to clear, and we had clean views of the landscape of sheep-infested squares of farmland, with the blue of the Tasman hinting to us from the west and the South Pacific beckoning to us from the east and announcing that while no man may be an island some nations were. In New Zealand, despite all the acreage of field and hill and forest that makes up the North Island, and all the mountains and great lakes and pasture land and vineyards of the South Island, water is never far away, falling from the sky, gushing from the rock face, gathering in vast lakes, and always, always surrounding you no matter where you are, at home or out on the road. Stand anywhere in this buoyant country and it is like standing on the deck of a nation-size ocean-going vessel moving through time and great seas.

That's what the earliest immigrants to New Zealand discovered. Over a thousand years ago, the first Maori explorers paddled their giant oceangoing canoes—seven of them, as the myth would have it, each carrying members of a different tribe or sub-tribe—across the Pacific to shelter here in what is now called the Bay of Islands, on the northeast coast of the North Island. They described their landfall at the bluff now known as Cape Brett as Tiritiri o te Moana, or the Gift of the Sea. The morning after our own arrival my wife and I set out on a small motor-driven catamaran from the dock at Russell (originally Kororareka, the first settlement in New Zealand), jaunty Kiwi skipper Pete Stuart at the helm, slapping along on the slight chop to that same spot, Cape Brett, the easternmost point of the North Island.

The Maori explorers, like Captain James Cook and his crew, and the hundreds of English and American whalers who eventually found cheerful landfall at the Bay of Islands, had crossed thousands of miles of ocean to reach this haven. My wife and I, after our flight from L.A. and our four-hour drive from the airport, felt no less celebratory. Dolphins cavorted around our small boat. A warm wind off the South Pacific toyed with our hats and hair. Our guide, a chunky Maori man—and Vietnam vet—named Richard "Blandy" Witehera, chanted a prayer to his ancestors as we started out on our hike along the ridge of one of the seven small peaks the Maoris view as representing each of the tribes who arrived in those original seven canoes.

Blandy led us in a climb of several hundred feet to the lighthouse at the top of the point, and along a series of goat trails, naming plants and trees as we walked as though he were cramming for an examination in the flora of Eden—here is the ponga or silver fern, there is the flax plant, and notice the manuka or tea tree, and also the ti kouka, the so-called white-flowering cabbage tree that lends a tropical look to the shorelines and hillsides and whose shoots Captain Cook's crew nibbled on and deemed cabbage-like in taste. Some hours later, at the end of our exhilarating walk along the sacred ridges, we descended to the meadow above Deep Water Cove where Blandy chanted another set of prayers on the occasion of our successful walk. Pete sailed up in the catamaran and we climbed aboard and more than nibbled—devoured is more like it, after our hours of tramping—a lunch of fresh oysters, mussels, and lobster—they call it crayfish down here—he'd just hauled up from the bottom of the cove.

We were now the actors in our own little cinema of travel—two American wanderers, fleeing winter in the northern hemisphere, find themselves at large in a geologically phantasmal nation with a dramatic history—down near what one writer has called "the last curve of the earth…" Cut next to Kerekere Beach, our original destination, where the Waitakere Hills meet the ocean, a vertiginous drive down winding roads to the place where the imported piano of the film of the same name sat unattended on a vast strand of black volcanic sand, washed by the incoming tide and guarded at either end by two monstrous chunks of three-story-high rock.

Oh, movies, oh, illusion! Where were Holly Hunter and Harvey Keitel, she the mute immigrant from England, he the exotic Maori loner, the ill-fated lovers in that wonderful down-under romance? Where we walked in the sea-wracked remains of a recent high tide, marveling at the outsized nature of this fantastically beautiful location, young parents pushed baby carriages across the sand and weekenders from Auckland, many shirtless despite the constant wind off the ocean, chugged beer and played American rock-and-roll on their boom boxes while Japanese tourists shot at each other with fancy cameras against the rough spray and bass notes of the surf.

The gargantuan vistas dwarfed the scattered groups of temporary visitors to these old shores. Such beauty heaped on beauty! This small country can overwhelm you with its vistas, as if the gods of tectonic plates had said after wrenching the islands away from the pre-Cambrian super-continent of Godwanaland, we have sent you to a lonely part of the globe, surrounded by water and far from almost everything, so we will give you more sublime sights at home than any other country on the planet.

This truly came home to me one morning, when, with the Southern Alps, the South Island's main mountain chain, to the east of us and the forest leading to the sea to the west drifting in and out of clots of fog and sheets of rain, we decided to face the elements. Stopping at the headquarters of Alpine Guides in the hamlet of Fox Glacier, we pulled on winter gear and boots and packed up some sandwiches from a nearby café, hoping that the rain would stop long enough for us to make a picnic on the ice. We followed our guide, a handsome young literature student named Jonathan Hatteral (born in Paris, and raised in Tasmania) over a trail of rocks and around boulders toward the foot of the glacier. No talk of global warming here. We shivered as the rain grew heavier and the air took on the nearby chill of the glacier, and Jonathan explained that this river of ice that stretched down from among the peaks of the Southern Alps, after retreating for some decades, was now inching forward again toward the sea, a few miles to our west.

We were inching mountain-ward, overtaking a few other tourists, some in flip-flops and coatless, feckless folk from elsewhere in the world, who were completely unprepared for the rain and chill, and admiring the huge rocks that the ice had deposited in the old riverbed when it had made its former retreat.

"So strange here," I said over the noise of the rain, "the juxtaposition of this ice in the middle of this rain forest. I've never seen anything like it."

At which Jonathan, an accomplished climber for whom our little jaunt of a couple of hours over rocks must have seemed like the equivalent of afternoon tea, quoted Proust: "Life consists not in seeing new things but in finding new ways of seeing…"

"So strange here," I said again, "this talk of Proust while climbing toward that."

And I gestured toward the face of the glacier, now quite near, with its blue-purple light emanating from the interior of the ice.

Within minutes we reached the massive frozen flow, and Jonathan chipped away some fragments for us to hold.

Studying this chunk of old ice in my hand, I asked, "How long ago had this piece here from the face of the glacier been high up on the mountain?"

"Decades," Jonathan said. "Or perhaps a century ago. Or, say, as long ago as Proust's work is long."

The rain grew heavier. Having ventured this far in our climb, would we now put on our crampons and ascend the set of stairs carved in the ice to the surface of the glacier itself and make our picnic?

No, the rain would make the bread—and us—too soggy, so we began our descent, leaving the mysterious inner ice-glow behind us, worrying our knees in the climb back down toward sea level, and, when we reached the Alpine Guides office, drying off and spreading out our lunch, delicious omelet sandwiches chock full of white-bait, the local variety of smelt. Tired and hungry from our climb, we talked through mouthfuls of egg and fish about reading and the news and the weather and love and life, the kinds of things that give you comfort when you want to avoid the subject of what wonderful new sublime sight you can see next.

I looked at my wife and she looked at me.

This tiny country was beginning to offer us too much to do— and we hadn't even considered its indigenous sport of bungee-jumping or been lured by parasailing and trout fishing and deep-sea fishing and snorkeling and body-rafting down sheer canyons flush with hard-gushing rivers. After a starlit overnight stay on board a hundred-foot power-and-sail vessel on the ancient fiord of

Milford Sound—and after that bumpy ride toward Paradise—we decided that we needed to take a breather.

We settled in for a couple of days at a splendid lodge just east of the resort town of Queenstown, on the shores of Lake Wakatipu. The proprietors, two middle-aged men from L.A. who dreamed their way out of California and into the construction of a comfortable haven for travelers and tourists between the huge lake and the Crown range, left little to be desired in the way of comfort. My wife and I lay in bed, switching the satellite TV system back and forth between CNN worldwide business news and the enticing trailers on the Maori cable channel. At the edge of dusk we walked up to the top of the hill behind the lodge and watched a farm herd of deer race back and forth across their darkening pasture.

But we just couldn't sit still. Life in Kiwiland had become too much like a beautiful waking dream. So on a pleasant sunlit afternoon we drove a few miles east up into the foothills to the old gold mining camp of Arrowtown, where thousands of desperate men once panned for the sparkling ore in the Arrow River. Park your car just off the main street and within three minutes you can stroll down to the rushing stream that held so many hopes and destroyed so many illusions.

There's movie gold there, too, if you want to look for it. Head upriver about fifty yards, as Ian Brodie suggests in that guidebook to the filming of *The Lord of the Rings*, and you can wade in the prototype of the mythical Ford of Bruinen, where dark horses and dark-cloaked riders paused and reared, and then roared across the river, in search of a powerful ring. By then we were so caught up in that dreamy slower-paced story we were making with our real lives that we chose the other direction, walking downstream, on the path beneath the sheltering beeches, along the slow-rushing, jade-tinted waters of the Arrow, at home with ourselves, and yet happy to be meandering along in another world. No matter how far we tramped or climbed or drove or sailed we would never reach Paradise, we knew, but here, there, everywhere in this marvelous country, we had at least caught a glimpse of it.

Originally published in Gourmet

THIRTY-FIVE PASSAGES OVER WATER

1—On board the Arahura (which, in Maori, means Pathway to Dawn), the imposing steamer-size car/passenger ferry from Wellington, North Island, New Zealand, to Picton, South Island, New Zealand—this past winter. I don't know that we've been happier (knock on wood, as my dear late mother used to say). The weather was fair, bright sun, and once the large auto and passenger ferry pushed out of Wellington Harbor—all the colorful houses smiling down at us, the façade of an Oceanian Trieste—it churned around the point into the Cook Strait where we met head-on a strong chill breeze, reminding us of where we found ourselves, along the forty-first parallel, facing south toward Antarctica, where the waters of the South Pacific rushed to embrace and meld with the waters of the Tasman Sea.

I had a goal, to write a travel story about this small but fascinating dual-island nation, and K. was traveling with me. This was our lovely life together, sometimes bending toward my work, sometimes, on those extraordinary evenings when ten months of her work bloomed in twelve minutes on stage when dancers performed her choreographic creations, inclining toward hers. Who knows where we'll be when you read this, dear stranger or friend—under the ground or under the water, our ashes long scattered to milder winds than these? (If anyone at all will read this!)—but know that as far as we have traveled it has been good.

Standing on the captain's bridge of that ferry, a privilege bestowed on us by virtue of my assignment, we knew no better course than to go where the captain would lead us, and enjoy the moment-to-moment amazements of the three-hour voyage. Here a leaping pod of dolphins! A pod of clouds sailed above us as if in some sort of mirror image of how we moved along the water. All brightness now upon the waves. It was summer, when the powerful currents of the Strait were less fickle than in other seasons.

This meeting of the two oceans—ferries had gone down in storms here twice in the last century—nothing like it in the northern hemispheres. The embrace of the ferocious flows, where one begins the other ends. A love affair of fierce currents. The kind of love that comes in youth, when you know nothing and feel that you have an eternity, or later in life when you have almost everything and know that you will lose it. That kind of ferocity! Those clouds seem to descend, and where it was clear, suddenly we're seeing through a mist. Storms come up like this, and boats go down. But we press ahead, blithely, the radar showing nothing but blissful emptiness ahead. And then the fog cleared and we caught sight of the other side, the upper coast of the South Island, a line of tree-strewn cliffs and small fiords and channels. And K. and I turned to each other, holding hands like children about to play a game, and felt the pleasure of knowing we were almost there, wherever we were going.

2—December, six years before: on board the Royal Viking Sun, embarking from Rio de Janeiro, a voyage that began for us in great happiness. To dance with the samba school while in port! And then to sail out along the Copacabana and turn north along the coast to stop at Bahia, the colors of the houses there, the sway of the way the people walk! And soon, in a few days, our destination is the town of Belem, where the Amazon spills into the Caribbean, a dream of mine born of reading novels and histories and maps— to reach Belem.

Nothing more elegant on the water than this cruise ship. Only four hundred passengers and four hundred crew. Carefully appointed cabins, lovely dining, the desserts, the wines. Who could have traveled this way ever before in history? No king or Roman emperor could have found such comfort and ease on the ocean. Modern life, modern times, the fruits of democracy, where anyone—who can pay for a ticket of passage—may be treated like royalty!

Though we are guests of the shipping line, since I'm giving four lectures in exchange for our passage, so sort of a court jester, to get a luxurious free ride on the ocean in exchange for intellectual entertainment. "The Idea of Paradise" in Latin American literature—"The Nature of Brazilian Fiction"—these are the kind of confections I'm purveying on this voyage.

What did Columbus seek? How fearful was he when he made his first voyage? What did he find? How did he express it in his letters? To what metaphorical illusion was he in thrall? And us? What is our metaphor of America? What do we think of where we are, where we are going?

At the first talk, about twenty people gather—not bad, I suppose, twenty out of four hundred interested in such matters. That's about right, I figure. There were two hundred came out for the samba dancers on our night in Rio and a number of the older audience members walked out. Too risqué! Oh, the haunches on those women, the sway, the sway!

No one walks out of my talk. Do I sway! Does my language sway? In the last row of the ship's small movie theater an elderly man nods off.

We sail along about two miles off the coast. At night the lights of towns off the port side hold steady but remote while the stars overhead seem close at hand. But try to reach for one! Off starboard, the lamps of small fishing boats play in and out of the waves. What a life that must be, swaying on the waves all night, fishing for what comes from the deep!

K. and I walk the deck, around and around. There's that attraction, the call of the sea. Come in, come in, so easy to climb over the rail and jump. We hold each other close through the night.

Five days out, in the early morning, a telephone call comes by way of satellite. My brother calling from New Jersey to say that our mother has died, all the wood she knocked worn through.

We disembarked at a beach town, waited for the next flight out to São Paulo, connected on the overnight flight to Miami, connected on an early morning flight to D.C.

Sailing, disembarking, waiting, flying south, connecting, flying north—while my mother's lungs slowly filled with fluid. And the fishermen ran their lines into the South Atlantic deep. And the lights of cities winked on and off, and the stars held steady. At least at this distance.

3—Summer, twelve years before: on the ferry from Port Angeles crossing the Strait of Juan de Fuca, our destination Victoria, British Columbia, in the company of my dear friend Victor Perera (when he still had another eleven years to live). Calm summer weather, easy crossing, with Victor, a whale-watcher to the point almost of lunacy, leaned off the bow, on the lookout for orcas.

We spent an afternoon in Victoria, wandering the streets, enjoying the odd mix that western Canadians make, of white and yellow and brown skins. And then back again on the ferry before dark, with Victor straining yet again to see the orcas he knew—knew!—were swimming in the currents tearing now out to the Pacific. Yet none rose to the surface to salute him.

4—After all these years, growing up near New York City, living there a number of years, I finally take the Circle Line Tour around Manhattan, chugging around this island where I first dreamed some of my best dreams.

5—Late summer, 1985. In Helsinki with my son, on our way to Russia, to track my father's footsteps from Leningrad to Kiev and across Central Asia to Khabarovsk, filling in the stories that he had told me when I was a child in New Jersey. This is our first stop, a layover before boarding the express train the next day to the Finland Station in Leningrad. We wander through Helsinki, stroll down to the harbor, take a harbor ferry to the zoo, which is situated on an island in the harbor. For lunch we eat reindeer burgers.

An acquired taste, I suppose. That night, from the window of our hotel room, we watch the drunks sway down the street and fall, one by one, into the roadway, where slow-moving automobiles drive around them, as in some slow-motion obstacle course. In the morning they are gone.

Weeks and weeks later, all the way on the other side of the great northern landmass with Scandinavia and Russia in the west and the Kamchatka Peninsula to the east, J. and I take a Russian steamer from the port of Nahodka to Yokohama. The large cliffs to the south and north of the port mirror the coast of Big Sur, and it seems as if our two regions—northern California and eastern

Russia—are two parts of the same whole, having broken off and drifted apart as the Pacific ran between.

Russia soon fades into the mist as we steam into the Sea of Japan, where once my father ditched his Red fighter plane and sat on the wing, waiting to be rescued by whatever ship first passed by.

Two days and two nights we're churning toward Yokohama. The beds are too small and the bathrooms stink and the food is spare. At night J. plays his DJ mix on the sound system in the lounge and Russians and Japanese and a few stray travelers from elsewhere like ourselves jump and sway to the rock and roll. Later at night we stand at the stern and watch the Sea of Japan recede into the darkness and I wonder if in some off-continuum of time my father might still be out there, waiting to be rescued.

6—1972. (All that long ago!) Mid-autumn. In New England the leaves have fallen. In southern Mexico the turbid air holds Caribbean moisture and the humidity feels as thick as the ocean. M., my second wife and I, have put winter behind us and traveled (separately) to Mexico and have rendezvoused in the Yucatan capital of Merida. In a hotel across from the Parque de las Madres, Mothers' Park, we make our base, venturing out to stroll through the city and to visit the nearby Mayan ruins.

In the face of these pyramids and ballfields, towers and steps, and moats and sun-stones, I find myself in absolute confusion. No more looking to Europe for genius and greatness! Here was a civilization complete unto itself, with architecture as beautiful and impressive as any Parthenon! And waiting here for all of our ancestors to travel over water from Europe and Asia to make this encounter! And if their gods seem more cruel than the ones our forefathers carried with them from the Old Country, their wars— Flower Wars!—seem less cruel.

All of this is on my mind as we embark on the motor launch

that passes for a ferry for the trip from the tip of the Yucatan to Isla Mujeres, a small crescent-shaped island a few miles across the water. A boy only a bit older than my son serves as captain and crew. He's wearing a captain's cap and a shirt with zebra stripes. A dozen of us climb on board and without a word the boy revs the engine and turns the craft into the waves. Over and heave, heave and over, the rhythm of this (mercifully) short journey makes me bend my knees and sway to the pattern of it.

Warm salt wind, noxious fumes from the engine, hypnotic heave and forward flow, the sun bears down, my nerve crashes as I wonder about this child steering us across, all the way to the island.

That night, in a small hotel made of concrete blocks, with the noise of the surf and the cackling of chickens in the yard below, our first daughter was conceived.

7—Water comedy. Sailing from San Pedro Harbor, on a cement boat, with friends, including my old college pal D. Our destination is Catalina Island. But the Pacific is not so calm, and D., looking like a pale beached whale, goes below, sicker than sick, and so we turn around and head back to shore.

8—Sweet views over water, the sun, the fog, the summer I lived in a friend's house in Sausalito and traveled on the ferry back and forth across San Francisco Bay from Marin to the city.

9—Sailing on a forty-two-foot ocean racer around the bays and inlets of Maine, my first father-in-law at the wheel, nights cold enough in July to turn on the inboard heat.

Our route takes us from Maine to Boston Harbor and back. Oh, my then very young son on board, sometimes standing at the wheel, the picture of boyhood bliss!

10—A hurricane is rolling north along the Atlantic Coast, the weather report says.

That's the time my father-in-law loved to set sail, Air Force general, nicknamed "Sailor," pushing out into the winds.

I held the wheel while he worked the sails.

"Did you ever read a book called *Moby-Dick?*" I shouted to him over the rising roar of the storm.

"I don't read books like that," he called back to me. "I live them!"

11—First time out on the small sailboat, skipping around Chesapeake Bay, and we capsize. Vast tribes of jellyfish sting my buttocks and legs. No more small boats for me!

12—A few years earlier. When I settled in to a job after traveling it was as an assistant editor at a trade magazine in lower Manhattan and I lived at home and commuted back and forth on the PATH train and on the Weehawken Ferry, back and forth, back and forth, and all that year and more, while there were a lot of girls in Manhattan to fool around with (because I was so unserious at that time that I didn't know enough to do more than that), nothing thrilled me as much as seeing the Manhattan skyline growing closer and closer as I traveled over water each morning.

13—Ten years earlier (continued): Returning on board a Holland-America liner from Liverpool to New York. Befriended an English advertising executive who was on holiday with his girlfriend. One night they got roaring drunk and at dawn went up on deck and while I watched—I was then in an early stage of the voyeurism that drives many, if not all, writers—they proceeded to throw dozens of deck chairs overboard. That same evening, a Chinese American girl from Chicago climbed up into my upper bunk and we fooled around. I didn't like her perfume, but I liked her touch. That and the endless rows of waves is all I recall of that voyage.

14—Ten years earlier (continued): At the Dead Sea, a Chagallesque moment as a fat man in bathing trunks and derby floats on his back playing gypsy tunes on an old violin. I try to swim but merely float myself.

15—Ten years earlier (continued): Traveling in Greece. An afternoon at the Parthenon impresses me, though I don't fully understand why. (When I was in grade school I made a model of the Parthenon out of hundreds of toothpicks!) Drunk in Athens. Visit to a brothel in Piraeus, but only to ogle. I have a brief sexual encounter with an English girl, a nurse on holiday. She teaches me to sing "I've Got a Lovely Bunch of Coconuts…" I drink ouzo and shoot pool.

After some weeks I board a steamship in Piraeus and sail to Haifa. My father, a refugee from Red Russia, wants me to visit Israel, and so I made the two and a half(?)-day trip across the Mediterranean, taking my meals on board with an Israeli family whose daughter was working at a kibbutz near the Dead Sea. They urged me to visit her. I promised I would, seeing myself as the hero in a drama in which I would travel to the desert and find the girl and win her.

The voyage itself was unremarkable. What did I know then—nothing!—about Odysseus' ten-year voyage over these same Mediterranean waters, struggling, yearning to return home? I was outward bound, sailing away (flying away, running away) from family, and myself!

16—Ten years earlier (continued): I had been living in a fishing village in Fuengirola in a small house on the beach, near college friends, trying to write fiction, and since whatever I was producing wasn't satisfactory I got the idea that I should travel.

First, I took the ferry across the Straits of Gibraltar, between the great gates of Europe to the north—the Rock—and Africa, the cliffs at Tangiers—to the south past which the Atlantic and Mediterranean currents flushed and revved. We rode into the sun. I drank the wind. It was lovely, it was Life.

I spent several weeks wandering about the casbah in a state of marijuana-induced delirium and then returned on the ferry to Spain. That wasn't enough travel, physical or mental, to satisfy me.

I booked passage on a ship that sailed from Gibraltar to Piraeus. I have no memory of this voyage at all except the astonishing vision of swinging out into the sea with Rock receding into the distance. Or am I just imagining what I would like to have noticed?

17—Passage from New York to Rotterdam, the autumn before, on a Holland-America ship. After working for a number of months as a toll-taker on the New Jersey Turnpike, I had saved enough money to travel. I was going first to meet a Dutch girl whom I knew at college, who was now working as a *Time* magazine stringer in Amsterdam. She took me on a trip along the canals and my mind floated away from her, thrilled with the particulars of where I was and where I was going, but pulling away from her even as we made our reacquaintance. She had a room on the top floor of a narrow house, and we climbed the steep stairs together once or twice. And after a night when I awoke screaming from a nightmare about my mother—who thought to ask why?—I made my excuses and took the train to Paris and then on down to Spain, where friends from college had taken up residence. From a small house on the beach at Fuengirola, I gazed out toward North Africa, wondering what it would be about.

18—One summer earlier, I returned from Liverpool to New York on a Holland-America liner, after two months of kicking around Europe, from France to Germany—and Denmark and back to Germany again on board a small auto ferry that churned placidly across the water. My first ferry ride since New Jersey days. A rougher ride on the back of a friend's motorcycle from Paris to La Rochelle. Traveled by car with friends from Paris to Valencia. Rode the trains.

19—First voyage out, from New York to Le Havre, between my junior and senior year at college. All the vast expanse of ocean all around us, it opened my eyes, it made me wonder about where I had been and where I was going. I met a girl on board, a dark-skinned Jewish girl from Brooklyn, with smoky eyes and puffy lips. We spent some time watching the endless waves and when we went below I followed her around like a puppy and she was kind to me, but kept her distance. Le Havre at sunrise, a million splinters of light reflected from the windows of the city.

20—The strong salt stink, the rise and fall of the stern of the boat, the clank of the deck when a car rolled aboard. The ship's whistle, the chugging of the engines. Our young hearts raced with the expectation of the journey, as short as it may have been.

Excursions on the ferry that ran from the foot of Smith Street in my hometown of Perth Amboy, New Jersey, to Tottenville, Staten Island (Borough of Richmond), New York City, New York—these were special. When I was very young and my parents wanted to make an outing of a Sunday we sometimes rode this small ferry across the Arthur Kill to Tottenville, across the water on Staten Island. And back again. (My mother remembered taking this same little journey with her parents when she was a child.)

The ferry became our route of choice when a couple of us pals wanted to take a little trip to Manhattan, boarding the ferry to Tottenville, and then taking the Rapid Transit Train to the northern tip of Staten Island and then taking the larger ferry to the Battery, and back again. Though it was mostly on foot, and in cars, and on trains and buses, that I traveled most of my early life—cars being particularly appropriate since my father worked as an engineer on the General Motors assembly line in the plant in Linden, New Jersey, though the more I learned about his life, ships and airplanes would later seem just as apt, since he had crossed the

Pacific from where he was living in Shanghai, to San Francisco, in the late 1930s, after an adventurous early life as a pilot in Russia and the Far East.

21—Out beyond this particular point of land far enough you can see the beginning of the curve—periplum—and imagine how all this once made a paradise, deer walking down to the waterside, lapping quietly at the base of trees where the fresh water pooled after the tide pulled out, and turning their over-large heads now and then at the splash of a wave.

Otters dove for clams in the old bay, making their own wake. Sunlight, spring and summer heat nourished multiplicities of plants. Small animals chewed at the roots, birds pecked at seeds. Nothing vast had occurred here for thirty million years, all this land sloping gently toward the water. To the west a river flowed out of very old hills, but here it bled away into marshes before lapsing into the bay.

On the old sand, horseshoe crabs, looking like catchers' mitts on legs, walked sidewise toward each other to do battle or mate, and past the spit of land rang big schools of small fish. Imagine the peace, a million years at least of only animal noise and thunderstorms, the wind in the branches, the boom and crack and lightning hiss of rain above the trees, the wash of waves in winter winds, the snap and crash of ice in the coldest part of winter.

For a thousand years this point of land showed no special beauty, only the tranquility of its own solitude. From earthworm to owl, from roots to treetops, it held a pleasure all its own. It was young and it was ancient, it was spare and yet a miracle of spectacle in miniature in the plentitude of small creation: this particular point of land that had no name because no one lived here to speak one.

I don't know how it would have been, born into a town without a coastline. A river alone would have done, I suppose. Plenty of people live interesting lives growing up alongside rivers. But the beach, and the bay leading out into the great ocean, these elements to me made all the difference.

The ebb and flow of waters, the detritus, flotsam, treasures left behind on the sand, the marine life, fresh water and salt mingling in the tides, the sound of buoys on summer nights, bells, horns, the ships anchored within sight of our playlands: the hope this gives you as a child, there is almost no explaining.

On this particular afternoon I was the one in the stern, navigator, tourist, witness, yet still carried along on the adventure. The sky seemed all one perfect piece of light blue glass, without a cloud to mar its smooth and slightly glowing surface. Turn the world upside down and look up on it and you would have sworn that it was a bowl of glass blown by the master of the craft, no flaw, no streaks, not even an imperfect ray of reflected light, a bowl into which all of us might have slipped and slid, rolling to the bottom where we would have been prisoners forever since without sprouting wings we never could have scaled the sides to the lip and freedom.

But here we were, rowing on the bay whose waters were tufted with little white tops when a breeze blew up now and then but which remained for the most part calm, almost a lake where we boys could have our fun without the threat of deeper trouble that the ocean signified. The pull of the tide did not seem strong, not that we paid much attention to the surge of the tide, either coming in or going out. It was just a small rowboat, a simple outing for us, and tide was something that only seagoing sailors had to worry about.

Here was the layout of our little pond: on the opposite shore from the dock where we started out, the beaches of Staten Island, where we often played. And to the south of us on the far shore of the river lay South Amboy, with its rails and power lines and blackened wreckage of the piers and jetties that one late afternoon some years before, more than half our lives at that time it seemed, a vast explosion had ripped apart flesh and wood and stone. Some terrible things had happened that day, and the waves of that explosion still rolled out across the years, though at that time and that place we couldn't know all the shock, all the story, only those parts that had directly touched ourselves. And as for the present, we were rowing! rowing! and tragedies grand or pathetic were things we left behind on shore.

We were rowing! to where the bay widened at the confluence of the Arthur Kill and the Raritan River. Oil tankers and freighters dropped anchor here to wait for tugboats to tow them up the kill under the Outerbridge Crossing and past Outerbridge Reach to the docks at Port Newark or west upriver to the refineries where their dark holds full of oil would be siphoned off into the huge tank farms that bordered the town just beyond the road bridge to South Amboy. Out beyond the tankers the harbor light stood rooted in rocks in the center of the bay. (I'd heard stories that one magical winter morning early in the century, when my own mother's mother had been only a little girl herself, the water had frozen to a depth so thick that people from town rode their sleighs all the way out to the light. But in this warm weather now, with the current tufted white in the slight wind, that freeze seemed only a dream or a miracle no one would ever wish for!) Beyond the light lay the ocean, Europe, Africa, places we knew only from our geography books and the movies we saw each weekend uptown on Smith Street.

But the tankers anchored before the light were like textbooks in themselves, a catalogue of countries and flags, German ships and Nordic ships and Japanese ships and Arab ships and African ships, bearing flags with stars and crescents and animals and scimitars and mountains and clouds and fire and fountains, a field of flags in the air above the slightly undulating waters of the bay. And sailors, seamen of all kinds, in uniform whites and blues and greys and in work clothes of various hues light and dark and sometimes shirtless and sometimes wearing round hats and square caps and smoking cigars and cigarettes and pipes and working on deck or fishing off the stern or swimming off the bow.

Sometimes we'd approach these ships, rowing as close as we could without endangering ourselves with the possibility of a sudden wave heaving us against the side of a vessel or against the huge dark mossy chains that ran from the ship into the water where the anchor had been dropped. Sometimes there'd be no one on deck and we'd row around the entire length of a tanker watching for activity in the lower portholes or on one of the lower decks. And now and then we'd be rewarded with the sight of a man in a chef's hat peeling vegetables or two or three sailors throwing a ball back and forth or one of those lone fishermen or a few divers. The divers, the swimmers were the ones we liked best, because now and then they spoke to us in greeting, calling out in their native tongues or once in a while flinging a heavily accented *hello* or *good morning*.

It embarrassed me when my foreign-born father spoke this way in front of my friends, but out here on the water, with these strangers—adventurers, sailors!—talking in their odd accents, the world felt like a story in which I was playing a principal role.

"Hi!" we'd call out to the men.

"Hello!" they'd sometimes call back.

"Hey!" I'd shout. "You there!"

All the while we were rowing to keep ourselves within hailing distance, bobbing up and down in the flow, hoping to keep this tenuous contact with visitors from other shores.

"You like to swim?"

"Oh," a sailor called to us from where he stood leaning out on the anchor chain, his long hair plastered down over his neck like a seal's, "Oh, yes! Yes!"

And another would splash up to the anchor chain, grab hold, hoist himself up, and call to us, "You come, too? Yah? Yes?"

And we'd laugh and smile and hold up a hand to show that we considered ourselves helpless, capable of rowing out here but not of diving off into the heaving waters.

And then the wind would shift and turn us about and we'd get caught up once more in the business of rowing, and the swimmers would wave to us from the giant anchor chain, and we'd watch them over our shoulders as we pulled back toward shore until the sailors disappeared against the darkness of the water and the ship itself in sunlight seemed to brighten out as if in flame spreading against the larger sky. And we rowed back to shore and returned to our families in the houses where we lived, on the verge of, but not quite yet understanding, that land was not solid and houses were like ships, and time was like water, like a river, feeding into a great salt bay and the ocean beyond where eventually everything gathered, everything found and lost.

22—On my Uncle Joe's motorboat, puttering around Greenwood Lake, an elongated freshwater body that straddles the North Jersey, southern New York State border. Around the dock at the lower part of the lake kids splash and swim. In the upper reaches the water glows, a dark green, and the trees loom more mysteriously as we approach the shore and then slide away.

There is my mother, who doesn't get along with Joe's wife. I hear them arguing about small things that loom large for them, what to fix for lunch, what to fix for dinner. My father is happy to be here with his brother, and my cousins, older, more water-wise, who take us out on the boat. (My uncle had traveled to America a full ten years before my father, across the Atlantic).

Night closes in, and from my place on a coat beneath a window in the large cabin through which seeps in large flows of cold night country air I listen to my parents in the other room, murmuring, murmuring (quarreling, about family, about who knew what back then at that time at that age?).

23—In the early morning of January 23, 1940, I swam out of my mother's womb and made landfall in Perth Amboy, New Jersey.

24—Back and forth on the Weehawken Ferry, my father traveled, on his way from Brooklyn to Perth Amboy, courting my mother.

25—In the late 1930s my father boarded a steamer and sailed from Shanghai to San Francisco. From there he traveled across the continent by train to New York City and lived for a while in Brooklyn with his brother Joe and sister-in-law Sadie and the kids. Some months later, after he had found his own place to live, he met my mother at a dance in Brooklyn.

26—Back and forth on the Weehawken Ferry, my mother traveled, to see her cousin Ethel in Brooklyn. That weekend, there would be a dance. She loved the dances.

27—After some months in Hokodate, Hokkaido, Japan, my father sailed to Shanghai and took a job flying in the China Mail Service.

28—My father, having ditched his stalled fighter plane in the Japan Sea, stood on the floating wing and squinted into the sun as a Japanese freighter approached.

29—As a young girl, my mother, holding her mother's hand almost all the time, rode the small passenger ferry to Tottenville and back again.

30—Her father, born in the Russian Pale, made a North Atlantic crossing as a child.

31—Her mother was born in New Jersey to a woman who made the North Atlantic crossing from Europe when she was a young bride, fleeing with her husband, who had killed a man in a political argument in their native Rumania.

32—Forty days and forty nights, Noah sailed his ark across the waters of the Flood.

33—The first of our ancestors, a naked fish with bulging eyes and stubby legs, crawled out of the sea, green saltwater spilling down its leathery sides, breathed the air, touched land, returned, and returned to breathe again.

34—Large landmasses shifted, swayed, reshaped and reformed—for a million, million years.

35—And the Lord moved upon the face of the waters and separated them upon the earth. And saw that it was good.

Originally published in the Antioch Review

READING THE ARCHIPELAGO

Last year, on a long flight from the United States to the southern end of the Indonesian archipelago (a part of the world I had never visited and had scarcely ever thought about before), I carried some books along with me to read. I can't recall now which books I took. But I do know what books I brought back.

A volume of Somerset Maugham's Far Eastern stories and some stories by Indonesian fiction writer Pramoedya Ananta Toer, which I bought at the Singapore airport. And after I arrived home and unpacked I went to my own bookshelves and to the library and bookstore to search for more fiction about the region; I found early Conrad, more Maugham, some mid-nineteenth- and twentieth-century Dutch fiction, and what little contemporary English, Australian, and American fiction there was on the subject of the Indonesian archipelago and the Malaysian part of the world. And a tetralogy by the same Pramoedya Ananta Toer.

After my visit, I was hungry to know more about the place. The few histories I had read of the region before leaving on my trip gave me what I took to be a reasonably solid background in the political and cultural past—the early history of life under the various Muslim and Hindu rulers who conquered the indigenous people of the archipelago, the effect of migration from other parts of south Asia, the lure of coveted spices that drew Western powers to colonize the region, the centuries of colonial rule, the torture of Japanese occupation, the post–World War II independence movement. But fiction, which still trumps history when it comes to putting you in a certain time and place, past, present, or future, would, I hoped, give me the feel of the real life of the region.

I had a hazy recollection of first stumbling on these matters a long time ago in my days as an innocent undergraduate reader in search of I knew not what when I picked up a volume of Conrad, and then forgetting about it. Safely home but with images of the Indonesian archipelago in all my waking thoughts and flooding my dreams, I felt driven to look back into those works where I first spied out the hazy horizons of the Java Sea and the coast of Borneo. So I went to Conrad again.

"The coast of Patusan...is straight and somber, and faces a misty ocean," he writes in *Lord Jim*. "Red trails are seen like cataracts of rust streaming under the dark-green foliage of bushes and creepers clothing the low cliffs. Swampy plains open out at the mouth of the rivers, with a view of jagged blue peaks beyond the vast forests. In the offing a chain of islands, dark, crumbling shapes, stand out in the everlasting sunlit haze like the remnants of a wall breached by the sea..."

Though most of the action takes place on rivers and in jungles, the novelist locates some important scenes near the coast, within easy view of a sailor or traveler. In the first two volumes of the Malay trilogy, which includes *Almayer's Folly*, Conrad's first, *An*

Outcast of the Islands, another early work, and *The Rescue*, a novel he wrote relatively late in life, much of the action takes place inland, on rivers and in jungles. The jungle description was among the first of that variety of landscape that I had read. "The brilliant light of day fell through the irregular opening in the high branches of the trees and streamed down, softened amongst the shadows of big trunks. Here and there a narrow sunbeam touched the rugged bark of a tree with a golden splash, sparkled on the leaping water of the brook, or rested on a leaf that stood out, shimmering and distinct on the monotonous background of somber green tints. The clear gap of blue…was crossed by the quick flight of white rice-birds whose wings flashed in the sunlight, while through it the heat poured down from the sky, clung about the steaming earth, rolled among the trees…"

The first word that comes to mind when you encounter passages such as these as a novice reader is exotic. Especially for a younger, newer reader, such descriptions serve to transport you to a location quite foreign, and rarely, if ever, visited. And, in fact, Conrad's novel, published in 1896, was received in this way in the *Bookman* where, as later critics have noticed, the reviewer compared his novel to "exotic" work by the French novelist Pierre Loti.

Conrad himself balked at the term, seeing the book in quite another light. In an author's note to a later edition, he responded to the *Bookman* critique by saying that he didn't think the charge of "exotic" was at all justified. "For the life of me," he wrote, "I don't see that there is the slightest exotic spirit in the conception or style of that novel. It is certainly the most tropical of my tales. The mere scenery got a great hold on me as I went on, perhaps because (I may just as well confess it) the story was never very near my heart. It engaged my imagination much more than my affection…"

The distinction the novelist himself makes between the "exotic" and the "tropical" is both interesting and useful. "Exotic" comes from horticultural usage and refers to a plant or flower introduced from another country. (It derives from the archaic term meaning something foreign or alien). Conrad's reviewer was probably using the word to mean something that is strikingly different, exciting or mysteriously different. And you can see why an English reviewer at the end of the nineteenth century might see it that way, given our current scant knowledge of the region that Conrad deploys as his setting and subject. (Though with British colonialism in its heyday at the time the book was published, the English were probably more aware of the Indonesian archipelago than most Americans are right now.)

Conrad didn't take the descriptive "exotic" as a compliment. He preferred "tropical," a more neutral term because it is simply the description of a geographical setting (one in which the climate is frost-free with temperatures high enough to support year-round plant growth), to the more weighted "exotic."

"Tropical" is simply a certain sort of geographical setting. It is scenery that, as Conrad put it, "got a great hold" on him. We find it first in *Almayer's Folly*, as in, for example, the scenes when Almayer's daughter Nina and the Balinese prince Dain make their way upriver by canoe:

"Over the low river-mist hiding the boat with its freight of young passionate life and all-forgetful happiness, the stars paled, and a silvery-grey tint crept over the sky from the eastward. There was not a breath of wind, not a rustle of stirring leaf, not a splash of leaping fish to disturb the serene repose of all living things on the banks of the great river. Earth, river, and sky were wrapped up in a deep sleep, from which it seemed there would be no waking. All the seething life and movement of tropical nature seemed concentrated in the ardent eyes, in the tumultuously beating hearts of the two beings drifting in the canoe, under the white canopy of mist, over the smooth surface of the river..."

This is thoroughly romantic stuff, the presentation of nature as if it has a hold over the observer because it possesses some sort of innate power, and that power is focused in the love between the young prince from the southern tip of the Indonesian archipelago and the Eurasian daughter of the European and his Malay wife.

When you look at it up close it seems the opposite of exotic, but something much more like the exultant representation of the natural world we find in Chateaubriand and in Cooper's Deerslayer novels—nature as holy place, nature as temple. To be fair, Conrad does try to represent the inhabitants in less romantic fashion, sketching out his Muslim—local rulers and Arab traders—characters with as much careful detail as he can muster. There's no escaping, though, the stiffness of the dialogue and the woodenness of the scenes.

The early-nineteenth-century Dutch writer on Indonesian themes, Edward Douwes Dekker, known by his pen name "Multatuli" (Latin for "I have suffered greatly"), doesn't do much better. His 1859 landmark novel *Max Havelaar: Or the Coffee Auctions of the Dutch Trading Company*, which some contemporary Indonesian writers have called the *Uncle Tom's Cabin* of Indonesian literature, precedes Conrad's first novel by about forty years. It admits us into the corrupt world of Dutch colonial rule in Java. But it doesn't deliver much of a sense of place, the kind of setting that Conrad was striving to create.

The book presents a taxonomy of Dutch rule and peppers the text with Malay words and phrases, but the actual visible world of what was then called the Dutch East Indies is usually referred to in general ways—we hear a lot about the "vegetation," as in this passage describing the land just beyond Havelaar's

compound: "This ravine had always been a source of vexation...
The vegetation, which grows rapidly enough everywhere in the
Indies, was especially rank there, owing to the constant accretion
of ooze from the river. In fact it was so luxuriant that, even if the
water had advanced or receded violently enough to uproot and
carry off the brushwood, very little time would have been required
to cover the ground again with all the scrubby plant life which is
so difficult to keep the compound clean..."

Multatuli seems at first to take a position on the side of exotic
rather than the tropical. As when he has his narrator describe
Max Havelaar's house. "You would be mistaken," he says, "if you
thought of a house in Java in European terms...In nearly every
case, houses in the East Indies have only one story. This may
appear strange to the European reader, for it is characteristic of
civilization—or what passes as such—to think everything strange
that is natural..." But then he reverses himself and states that he
will eschew "picturesqueness" and gives a geometric description
of a Javanese compound and its many outbuildings, including a
diagram of their placement. Part polemic, part satire, the rather
stiffly conducted novel, despite its historical importance, ends up
being quite unsatisfying to a contemporary reader.

After Multatuli, writers belonging to the colonizing culture of
the archipelago kept trying to portray the foreign place it had made
its own. The turn-of-the-century Dutch novelist Louis Couperus
produced, among his other works, a more pleasing attempt at
making fiction with an Indonesian setting, a novel titled *The Hidden
Force*. Unlike Multatuli, who went to the Dutch East Indies as a
young man, Couperus spent part of his childhood on a family
plantation in Java. When he writes about the place, he creates
deeply layered romantic fiction rather than the hard-edged satire
of the impassioned reformer. On the surface his subject is the

repressed life of a Dutch colonial official named Van Oudijck and his troubled marriage. In the execution of this story he attempts to allow the material of the buried life to emerge.

"The mysticism of concrete things on that island of mystery called Java...a hidden force lurks, slumbering now and unwilling to fight. Under all this appearance of tangible things the essence of that silent mysticism threatens, like a smouldering fire underground, like hatred and mystery in the heart..." Reading this novel is an interesting enterprise, if you have your eye out for passages such as this in which the novelist's sense of how the setting influences the character ranks as high as the movement of the story. Fortunately there's a secondary character in the novel, a Dutch woman named Eva Eldersma who is the wife of another colonial official, whose sense of her surroundings is quite similar to the novelist's. When Eva first arrived in the Indies she was filled with illusions, seeing everything "as a beautiful fairy tale, a story out of the Arabian Nights..." Eventually she comes to view the Indies in a different light, blacklight, one might call it. She feels "something strange, something she could not analyse, a certain mystery and dark secrecy, which she felt creeping softly over the land at night..." Ultimately her sense of the hidden mystery of her surroundings is superficial, "a vague voice of warning, no more than a whispering in the night that evoked poetic imaginings..." By the end of the novel, a wonderful precursor to E. M. Forster's *A Passage to India*, she and Van Oudijck experience the mystery more directly, yet they still cannot name it, referring to it as "That," which seems to me a direct statement on the side of the "exotic" view of the material.

The modern Dutch fiction writer A. Alberts chases after this same ineffable mystery in his story collection *The Islands*, with both more and less success. Originally published in Amsterdam in

1952, the book is an odd mixture of the romantic and the realistic, a series of stories that sometimes seem to be taking the measure of the Indonesian archipelago and at other moments appear to be creating their own private realm. In "Green," the first story in the collection, told as a series of journal entries by a Dutch colonial official who is slowly going mad, the latter seems clearly stated in its references to the King Arthur legend: "I am on my magic forest. I walk trunks...The ground is rocky...it is a marvelous forest... It is Time itself, I say, laughing. Ancient, green, and always the same..." And later he writes, "A great bare land with many stones, big stones, hilly, with hazy blue mountains in the distance... Stonehenge, maybe, where Merlin stayed..."

But as romantic as this approach appears to be, most of the other stories remain more anecdotal than suggestive, portraying eccentric local characters rather than creating a large visionary canvas. In Alberts's work the representations of life in New Guinea and Java seem to oscillate between the romantic visionary place that vaguely resembles the New World of Chateaubriand and the serio-comic gestures of Multatuli, but they still err on the side of the exotic.

Up until this point in my reading, I hadn't made any startling discoveries. Rereading the early Conrad turned out to be something of a disappointment, but then rereading books you devoured in your youth can sometimes produce that effect. I wish I could say that reading Multatuli and Alberts somehow made up for it, but that's not true. These two seem necessary when you're reading your way along the archipelago, and they certainly are essential to the development of Dutch literature, but they're not writers I would go back to.

The first real surprise and pleasure came with the *Far Eastern Tales* of Somerset Maugham. The stories themselves are straightforward, realistic depictions of, for the most part, British colonials in Malaya, now known as Malaysia, and adjacent locations. Many of them yield a certain poignancy as they highlight the common human dilemma of being a stranger in a strange world, with this situation writ large for the colonial expats in foreign climes. They treat the situation of marriage, of love and adultery, of men on the rise or on the way down in the bureaucratic colonial system, of women trying, off to the side of the world of men, trying to keep their minds and families intact. Writing squarely in the realistic tradition, Maugham produces a good old-fashioned gallery of credible characters, some likeable, some despicable.

Moreover, I found something really interesting at work within the reality of the characters' surmise, and that was an awareness of the first generation of fiction about the territory in which they live, mainly Conrad's. As when, for example, the widow of a colonial bureaucrat in the story "Before the Party" recalls early moments of her stay in Borneo. "From the novels she had read," Maugham writes, "she expected the rivers of Borneo to be dark and strangely sinister, but the sky was blue, dappled with little white clouds, and the green of the mangroves and the nipahs, washed by the flowing water, glistened in the sun. On each side stretched the pathless jungle, and in the distance, silhouetted against the sky, was the rugged outline of a mountain. The air in the early morning was fresh and buoyant. She seemed to enter upon a friendly, fertile land, and she had a sense of spacious freedom..."

Here Maugham seems to be taking a stand with Conrad, agreeing in principle with the master that his work is less exotic than it is reflective of its tropical settings.

In the long story "Neil MacAdam," an initiation tale about a young Scot (with a portentous name) who ships out from England for work in the jungles of Borneo, Maugham becomes explicit about the literary tradition with which his characters are conversant. The main character, who gives the story his name, meets up with a sexually aggressive Russian émigré woman, Darya Munro, and she toys with him in the following conversation.

"Tell me," she says, "what did you read on the journey, or did you only play deck tennis?"

"I read a lot of Conrad," MacAdam replies.

"That Pole," Darya says, launching into a tirade against the writer. "How can you English ever have let yourselves be taken in by that wordy mountebank? He has all the superficiality of his countrymen. That stream of words, those involved sentences, the showy rhetoric, that affectation of profundity: when you get through all that to the thought at the bottom, what do you find but a trivial commonplace? He was like a second-rate actor who puts on romantic dress and declaims a play by Victor Hugo. For five minutes you say this is heroic, and then your whole soul revolts and you cry, no, this is false, false, false."

Though he finds her passion on the subject appealing, young MacAdam doesn't agree. "There's no one who got atmosphere like Conrad," he says in rebuttal. "I can smell and see and feel the East when I read him."

"Nonsense," the woman responds. "What do you know about the East? Everyone will tell you that he made the grossest blunders. Ask Angus."

The captain, MacAdam's boss, offers his opinion. "Of course he was not always accurate…The Borneo he described is not the Borneo we know. He saw it from the deck of a merchant vessel and he was not an acute observer even of what he saw. But does it matter? I don't know why fiction should be hampered by fact. I don't think it's a mean achievement to have created a country, a dark, sinister, romantic and heroic country of the soul."

"You're a sentimentalist," the Russian woman says. And she tells MacAdam, "You must read Turgenev, you must read Tolstoi, you must read Dostoevsky…"

Essentially three views of Conrad are stated here. One—he makes us see! Two—no, no, he's a wordy mountebank. Three, he may not be accurate but he's got a wonderful romantic vision of place. It would be a mistake, of course, to impute any of these views to Maugham himself. The fiction writer casts his net into his time and pulls in his catch, a various and full spectrum of how people see the world. And this may have something to do with Maugham taking a stand on the side of the tropical rather than the exotic, the first major twentieth-century writer after Conrad to do so.

But the lure of the exotic persisted. Around the same time that Maugham was publishing his South Asian stories, Vicki Baum, a prolific popular novelist best known for her novel *Grand Hotel*, brought out a novel set on the Indonesian island of Bali. *A Tale from Bali*, published first in Baum's native German, appeared in an English translation in 1937, and employs incidents from the colonial period of Bali's past as the armature of the book.

It does offer Western readers a straightforward look at the Balinese landscape, if decidedly of the travelogue variety: "The life of Bali was unfolded before their eyes as they rode along. Rice fields in rounded terraces opened out and then contracted again and descended step by step to the deep gorges where rivers foamed over the rocks. Palm groves crowned the ridges of the hills, which rose one above another up to the Great Mountain, whose summit was veiled in two long, sparse, white clouds. The huge dark domes of wairingin trees contrasted with the jewel-like green of the fields and the tawny temple gateways stood beneath them…Naked children wearing large hats drove flocks of ducks along the dykes…Old men with faces like dancers' masks walked along with sticks to help them…Women came from field or market, carrying baskets or sheaves of rice or towers of coco-nuts or great pyramids of earthenware vessels on their heads. The habit of carrying loads on their heads gave them an erect carriage and a rhythmic step, and their breasts and shoulders were at once soft and muscular…And everywhere there was the sound of running water, that blessed sound of the island's teeming fertility…"

Baum's presentation of Balinese life and culture definitely stands on the side of the exotic. It remains throughout the novel highly stylized and punctuated with statements suggesting the writer's commitment to presenting the inhabitants as essentially primitive and simplistic creatures, as when, say, the character of Raka, an aristocratic dancer, says to his beloved, "You must imagine heaven just like Bali. Just the same. There are the same villages and temples and puris. Only that in heaven everything stands on its head… Bali is a reflection of heaven…what you see sparkling as stars are the tips of young plants hanging down towards us…" All of the Balinese characters, according to Baum, possess "a contentment the white man does not know…" Her use of historical material to the contrary, Baum's Balinese confection is really a costume novel passing itself off as history.

Nearly twenty years and two wars later, Graham Greene created, in *The Quiet American*, a political/historical thriller set in Southeast Asia, employing with quiet genius generous amounts of local color. Though the novel is etched with sharp detail, it is as much about Greene's obsessions with such questions as faith and adultery and love as it is about Vietnam. Is he writing "tropical" or "exotic" fiction? Because the main characters are mostly all Westerners, I lean toward calling the novel exotic, Greene's favorite motifs playing out against an unusual backdrop.

Another gifted English expatriate novelist, Anthony Burgess, focusing our attention on the Malayan states just to the north, tries to work from both inside the culture and without. In his trilogy of novels, published in 1964 under the umbrella title of *The Long Day Wanes*, the polymath novelist seems to have his eye on *Passage to India* as a model for a literally multi-cultural cast of dozens of sharply etched characters, British expats, Malays, Eurasians, Indians, Arabs, and Chinese among them, which means a cast of Christians, Muslims, and Hindus, colonialists, communists, and mystics. Of all the books I read up until this point, his were clearly the most underrated. In relation to the exotic versus tropical argument, his trilogy comes down a bit ambiguously on the side of the tropical.

He certainly makes his settings vivid enough, with a touch of irony in the voice that delivers them, as in this passage early on in *Time for a Tiger*, volume one of the trilogy: "...soon the dawn came up, heaving over the eastern edge like a huge flower in a nature-film. The stage electrician, under notice, slammed his flat hands on the dimmers and there was a swift suffusion of light. The sky was vast over the mountains with their crowns of jungle, over the river and the attap [palm-leaf thatched] huts. The Malayan dawn, unseen of all save the bilal [the muezzin] and the Tamil gardeners, grew and grew and mounted with an obscene tropical swiftness, and morning announced itself as a state, not a process."

Burgess, no slouch when it comes to incorporating what he knows into the texture of a novel (and showing off to good effect his Joycean sense of language and his knowledge of the local culture, as in a moment in *Time for a Tiger* when his main character, public school teacher Victor Crabbe, lies sleeping), adds history to the setting:

Crabbe sleeps "through the *bilal's bang* (inept Persian word for the faint unheeded call), would sleep till the *ban gbang* (apt Javanese word) of the brontoid dawn brought him tea and bananas. He slept on the second floor of the old Residency, which overlooked the river...The river Lanchap gives the state its name. It has its source in deep jungle, where it is a watering-place for a hundred or so little negroid people who worship thunder and can count only up to two. They share it with tigers, hamadryads, bootlace-snakes, leeches, pelandoks and the rest of the bewildering fauna of upstream Malaya. As the Sungai Lanchap winds on, it encounters outposts of a more complex culture: Malay villages where the Koran is known, where the prophets jostle with nymphs and tree-gods in a pantheon of unimaginable variety. Here a little work in the paddy-fields suffices to maintain a heliotropic, pullulating subsistence. There are fish in the river, guarded, however, by crocodile-gods of fearful malignity; coconuts drop or are hurled down by trained monkeys; the durian sheds its rich fetid smell in the season of durians. Erotic pantuns and Hindu myths soothe away the depression of an occasional accidia...Where the Lanchap meets the Sungai, Hantu is the royal town, dominated by an Istana designed by a Los Angeles architect, blessed by a mosque as bulbous as a clutch of onions, cursed by a lowering sky and high humidity...Victor Crabbe slept soundly, drawn into that dark world where history melts into myth..."

In Crabbe's waking world, the situation is reversed. Consider the case of the Abang, or royal ruler, of the territory of Dahaga where Crabbe and his wife reside. Royalty, we hear, is of course, a joke. "There was not a drop of royal blood in his well-set randy body. There were rajahs picking up a few dollars a month as school-teachers, tengkus working in shops. Back in the misty reaches of the annals of Dahaga—part history, part legend—some vigorous peasant had obtained a hold over a sultan senile or insane with tertiary syphilis, and the myth had come into being. He himself did not believe in the story of the descent from the faeces of a sacred bull, or in the magical accolade of the Ghost Princess, but he believed in the power of a tradition which could raise earth-red blood above that watery blue which ran in some of the lowliest channels of the State..."

Because of both Burgess and Greene, the level of what the reader can expect from Western writers approaching this particular subject matter—life in this part of the world—was certainly raised higher than ever before. Though not many Western writers focused directly on Indonesia. One of the few writing in English about the archipelago was Australian journalist Christopher Koch in his novel *The Year of Living Dangerously*. Koch sets his book during the period of Indonesia's 1960s anti-communist purges—a book best known because of the successful movie version with Mel Gibson and Sigourney Weaver. It is a novel akin to Greene's *The Quiet American* in its successful execution of a thriller-plot that creates an exotic setting populated by keenly portrayed local inhabitants. Despite his wonderful representations of the indigenous character of Billy Kwan and well-made passages about life in both Djakarta and the Javanese countryside, this non-Western non-archipelago writer nonetheless can tell the story only from the outside of the culture looking in.

Alas, North Americans have rarely attempted to do even this much. One of the few U.S. writers who has written well about this part of the world is C. S. Godshalk in her novel *Kalimantaan*, a historical fiction about British colonials in Borneo, published several decades after the Koch. A not-so-thrilling attempt came from Claire Messud in her first novel, *When the World Was Steady*, which divides itself between England and the island of Bali.

Though Messud has proven herself in subsequent books to be a writer with real narrative gifts, her first novel turned out to be quite disappointing. The Bali sections of her story about the estrangement and eventual confrontation between two sisters don't even measure up to the level of the costume fiction of Vicki Baum. An expedition up the slopes of the sacred volcano Mt. Abang turns out to be rather ordinary, and most of the references to the locations and customs of the Balinese setting are superficial in the extreme. Aside from a few nouns and place names the setting, for all of its possibilities, seems perfunctory, as in this passage as Emmy, one of the two English sisters who make up the main characters of the novel, follows "a web of paths through the [rice] paddies..." She could, she thinks, "return in time to witness one of her favourite quotidian moments: the duckherder crossing the paddies in his mollusk hat with a stick on his shoulder and a half-dozen jabbering fowl marching smartly in his wake...But she realized as she set out that the sun was lower than she had thought...it would be too late. She even contemplated going back to her room: when night fell in Ubud, the earth disappeared and everything was given over to the realm of the spirits, a dark world of shifting shapes and unknown quantities. That was what the local people believed..." Just in terms of the texture of the prose the passage doesn't hold up in comparison with similar pages in the work of either Maugham or Burgess.

As some of you may be thinking, my compiling of this reading list hasn't been completely scientific. But I'm working here on personal bibliography. There may be a few more novels, perhaps written by Australians or Japanese, about Bali or the larger archipelago, but I haven't found them. Perhaps I haven't looked hard enough. But frustrated by much of this reading by writers who come to this subject from the outside I finally turned to the indigenous fiction writers, mostly all contemporary, to see how the subject came to life in their hands.

And it was then that I understood how naive my reading project truly was, trying to read my way forward through time as if to dramatize for myself the "discovery" of this part of the world by writers mostly from the cultures that colonized the archipelago. Imagine if one were doing this about the subject of North America, reading British and French and Italian and Russian and Spanish and Latin American writers about the United States and Canada. Would anyone be surprised to learn just how simple and uncomplicated the fiction was when written by the outsiders, and how subtle and complex the indigenous literature was?

But the question of the exotic versus the tropical makes matters extremely dense with respect to nonnative writing about Southeast Asia, or perhaps about any developing country. If the fiction writer's task is, in part, to reveal the exotic in the everyday and the everyday in the exotic, the task is thus all the more difficult when, because of what we might call the shock of the foreign or the exotic, it's impossible to distinguish between the two modes. The exotic lends a certain blinding aura to the material. Just to report on it sometimes comes across to the writer, if not the reader, as the main task.

In an indigenous novel such as Mochtar Lubis's *Twilight in Jakarta*, first published in English translation in 1963, and one of the important works of post-colonial Indonesia, the exotic is only a dim memory for most of the characters. In the corrupt world of Lubis's Jakarta, as it is in most protest fiction, nature is mostly reduced to the basic human appetites and occasional references to rain and wind. The landscape is that of the sprawl of Jakarta, reproduced in the periodic "city reports" that in Dos Passos–like fashion punctuate the end of chapters. As in, "People sleeping under the bridge tried to protect themselves from the sprays of rain blown in by the wind, screening themselves with worn-out mats and praying that the rain would not turn into a downpour. And the people who slept in the big water-pipe that was waiting to be laid underground moved deeper inside, away from the opening where the rain was dripping in..."

Driven by ideology, the characters can't see nature for itself alone. For example, while flying over the Indonesian island of Sumatra on his return from a political conference, Murhalim, the Islamic organizer who spends the second half of the novel in debate with his communist friend Achmad and other ideologues, looks out the window and sees below him "tail and steep mountain ranges, valleys in greens and yellow, and from time to time the brilliant light of the sun...on the surface of the streams which gleamed in their winding course below. A yellowish-white road stretched through the countryside. From above it looked like a fine, smooth road. But Murhalim knew how it was in reality: murderous for vehicles, full of pot-holes, deteriorating with every passing year, never repaired and like a thorn in the people's flesh penetrating deeper and getting more painful all the time..."

From the perspective of these post–World War II Indonesian writers, society is almost nothing but potholes, though the Suharto government, under whose rule Mochtar Lubis spent a number of years in prison, insisted on maintaining the illusion of the smoothness of the road. Playwright and poet W. S. Rendra, author of "The Mastodon and the Condors," who bumped up against the censors for his openly tract-like poems, uses a familiar metaphor in "Song of the Bottle of Beer": "Where are the old roads / which used to link one village to the next? / They have been neglected, / broken up, and carried away...We are carried along by a civilization we cannot control, / in which our only function is to eat and shit, / we are powerless to create anything. / Is this as far as we go?..."

During the late sixties and continuing on into the seventies, while writers such as Mochtar Lubis and W. S. Rendra were writing, traveling, and sometimes serving prison sentences for publishing work critical of the post-Sukarno government, a remarkable aesthetic event was slowly building in a prison camp on the Moluccan island of Buru in the Seram Sea to the west of Sulawesi and north of Timor, more than a thousand miles from the Indonesian capital of Jakarta. The Java-born writer Pramoedya Ananta Toer, incarcerated by the Dutch from 1947 to 1949 for his role in the Indonesian independence movement, had been arrested by the Suharto government and while imprisoned for nearly two decades composed his remarkable tetralogy popularly known as the Buru Quartet.

The four novels, *This Earth of Mankind, Child of All Nations, Footsteps,* and *House of Glass,* comprise one of the most notable achievements in modern literature, an achievement that has remained, for the most part, hidden from the general readership in the West for, ironically, the very reasons that gave birth to its composition. The tetralogy begins as a traditional Bildungsroman, or novel of education, as the narrator, a bright young Javanese boy, enters the Dutch-run school system in the latter part of the nineteenth century. He introduces himself as Minke, a name given to him in anger by a biased colonial teacher, who dubs him "monkey" in order to dismiss his obvious intelligence in class. "My own name," he says, "for the time being I need not tell it..."

The first three volumes offer a detailed chronicle of Minke's progress in school, in love, and then in business, as a journalist, and then as a medical student and as political organizer and leader at the forefront of the Indonesian independence movement. Along the way, the reader receives an intense education in the manners of Indonesian family life, the mores of the colonial rulers, the effects of colonial rule, all of the elements of the archipelago's culture that lead to the formation of the character of its modern citizens. A large cast of characters passes through these pages (mainly Javanese and other natives of the archipelago, Eurasians, Dutch colonial residents, and Indonesian-born Dutch), and there is a cumulative effect, something akin to that of Anthony Powell's twelve-volume novel about the formation of twentieth-century English culture, *A Dance to the Music of Time*. Minke, of course, always stays in stage center, and as he begins to achieve some success as a political leader the figure of a native policeman named Pangemanann begins to shadow him.

In a turnabout remarkable in terms of the style and remarkable in terms of the story, *House of Glass*, the fourth volume of the quartet, in which we learn of Minke's ultimate fate, is narrated by Pangemanann himself (in fact, composed by him, with the last pages written down at the very end of the volume, so that the time of composition coincides in the end with the time of the story, a trope quite familiar to modern readers). The effect of this is startling. At the same time it creates new distance between the reader and Minke it introduces us into the mind of a willing and educated native co-conspirator in the Dutch colonial rule of the Indonesian archipelago. It also adds a new level to the story since Pangemanann midway through the novel tells us of a project he has been working on, the study of Minke's manuscripts, which have been confiscated from the writer-hero during his imprisonment.

If it weren't clear that his presence as narrator points up the leap from the incipient social realism of the first three novels to the self-reflexive modernism of the fourth volume, his response to

Minke's books certainly does. "It was my impression," he writes, "they were all connected. There was a rupture between *This Earth of Mankind* and *Child of All Nations* on the one hand and *Footsteps* on the other. I wasn't sure though whether these were parts of a genuine autobiography or not...I decided I would put aside some time to check out the details of the story against the reality of any relevant official documents..."

It's not entirely clear what "rupture" he discerns. Ironically, the "rupture" the policeman-narrator refers to seems akin to his own relation to the novels he's scrutinizing, since he himself as a character is a link among all the volumes. Despite what he describes as his own training as a reader of difficult modern fiction ("I was reminded of literature classes at high school," he writes... "It was a pity that I was never asked to analyze a French work of the same caliber as these manuscripts. I mean the same caliber in the sense of looking at these kinds of transformations in values, world outlooks, and social life itself..."), he can't see his own true relation to the tetralogy, his role as mediator between Minke and the society from which the writer is removing himself and between Minke and the reader.

In *Don Quixote, Part Two*, we learn of the publication of *Part One*, and this self-reflexive complication leads us into the world of the modern novel. Here, as one of the minor characters in the first volumes of the Buru Quartet begins to analyze the earlier novels, we see Quixote eased into the age of worldwide anti-colonial struggles. And the character of Minke emerges, in the eyes of Pangemanann, as a new order of man. "This man...was perhaps the only Javanese who had thrown off all his illusions, both as a Javanese and as an individual...Perhaps he was the first Javanese realist..."

What's so interesting and surprising, at least to this Western reader, is the coincidence of literary modernism and the ideology of twentieth-century anti-colonial independence struggles. This goes against most of the experience of our reading. Modernism usually eschews ideology. Social realism doesn't usually put into play the innovative techniques of modernism. So the effect here is extraordinary, as though *Man's Fate* were somehow rewritten by Julio Cortázar.

A second major surprise for me came along with this first discovery. I set out in search, I suppose, of the exotic, or at least a literature steeped in tropical settings. And I found a distinctive variety of super-realism, the effect, as I tried to explain just now, of the fusion of social realism and modernism. But in terms of the literature of the archipelago itself, in local terms, we might more correctly say, there is less of a surprise and more of a continuity. As Pangemanann himself puts it, after reading a manuscript by one of Minke's young apprentices in the struggle to free Indonesia from foreign rule, "it has that Multatuliesque spirit..."

In other words, it's about reform and progress, earmarks of Western culture, but presented here in local terms. As is the entire Buru Quartet. Though it is avowedly a homegrown work of art, the product, as Pangemanann from his peculiar perspective of intimacy and distance sees it, of a Javanese who has freed himself from Javanism, Pramoedya's masterwork ranks with the major fiction of the Western twentieth century (though it is not without its critics, particularly Mochtar Lubis, who, after Indonesia gained its independence from the Dutch, became a political nemesis of the author's and when the book was awarded the 1995 Ramon Magsaysay Prize attacked its creator as a communist and demanded that the honor be withdrawn or he would return his own 1958 Magsaysay Award). Immersing yourself in the tetralogy you discover a case of the exotic turned inside out, the culmination of centuries of colonialism and subsequent anti-colonial struggle, a landmark work and a watershed, and a bridge between the old way of life and the possibility that beckons both for the citizens of the archipelago itself and for all of us who, as we read the fiction from this hugely populated and still relatively misunderstood part of the world, come to know (as do people who travel by airplane, train, car, boat, bicycle, on foot—or by book) something quite valuable that had never occurred to us before.

Originally published in the Antioch Review

CODA: TWO OCEANS

Americans, Russians, Patagonians, Inuit, Hawaiians, and Hindus, we all share an inclination toward water.

Those who live inland, as Herman Melville has written, are drawn to creeks and follow them on an eventual path to the sea. "Say, you are in the country; in some high land of lakes," his Ishmael tells us. "Take almost any path you please, and ten to one it carries you down in a dale, and leaves you there by a pool in the stream. There is magic in it. Let the most absent-minded of men be plunged in his deepest reveries—stand that man on his legs, set his feet a-going, and he will infallibly lead you to water, if water there be in all that region. Should you ever be athirst in the great American desert, try this experiment, if your caravan happen to be supplied with a metaphysical professor. Yes, as every one knows, meditation and water are wedded for ever."

I know that for me, an Easterner, a Jersey boy, born near the water's edge—the Raritan River where it flows into Raritan Bay, which feeds into the Atlantic around the tip of Staten Island—our two national oceans have made a great difference in my life. The sand, the water (there at the bay's edge), sometimes salt, sometimes fresh, depending on the tide and river currents, whetted my appetite for more. I'll always remember the best early days near the Atlantic.

One particular afternoon I sat in the stern of a rented rowboat, navigator, tourist, witness, yet still carried along on the adventure. The sky seemed all one perfect piece of light blue glass, without a cloud to mar its smooth and slightly glowing surface. Turn the world upside down and look up on it and you would have sworn that it was a bowl of glass blown by the master of the craft, no flaw, no streaks, not even an imperfect ray of reflected light, a bowl into which all of us might have slipped and slid, rolling to the bottom where we would have been prisoners forever, since without sprouting wings we never could have scaled the sides to the lip and freedom.

I have written before about this passage over water, and I have to admit to my obsession with it, and my obsession with all travel over water. It takes me back so deep into myself, and back so far into time, my own lifetime and, if we believe the Jungians and the evolutionary biologists, back into the far distant past, when we all traveled out of the sea and crawled in our old amphibian selves upon the new steaming land.

(Yes, we probably do all have monkey or ape ancestors, but before them we had the lungfish, the air-breathing grandfather from whom we learned the ability to take in oxygen rather than water. Lungfish to apes to us, a multi-million year leap in time that makes our daily round from morning to afternoon to night seem what it is, something comparable to the life of a mayfly!)

But oh I loved the water. As children we splashed at the lapping surf and as adolescents we combed the beach, and dug pits and built fires and roasted potatoes, camped out, and stared out over the water, gazing, gawking at the repetition of the waves and the erratic sightings of ships. Even as children we proved the truth of Frost's good poem "Neither Out Far Nor In Deep" that "The land may vary more; / But whatever the truth may be— / The water comes ashore, / And the people look at the sea..."

These were our best days, racing along the line where water met land, finding shells and ropy strands of seaweed, dead fish in various stages of decay, and now and then a real prize—a starfish, with all its appendages intact!—a stone as pure as pearl!—a length of natural wood smoothed and cleaned by the relentless tide, so that it seemed more art than detritus. Running, dancing about like the tiny shore birds that danced away at our approach, we breathed into our growing lungs the cleansing iodine stink of a bay that led to an ocean that led to other oceans, circling the globe. Submerging our grasping hands, we could try to touch water that only weeks or months before had lapped at the beaches of England and Africa, of India and Arabia, of China and the myriad islands of the distant Philippines.

I remember these lovely days, when barefoot and wild, our gang splashed about as if in the celebration of that first lungfish's emergence on the beach. To take us in the right direction in time, the ancient horseshoe crabs scuttled past our toes, creatures that had not changed their form in a hundred million years or more.

I remember the worst days, too. The slate-gray Atlantic, waves breaking over my head, knocking me down, filling my nose and throat with salt. You might call it fun for a child to play in that rough surf on the beach at Asbury Park, New Jersey, or slightly farther south along the sand. I splashed about there, when I didn't know any better, trailing along in my parents' lives. This was their brief vacation, a few days at the shore.

"The shore..." That's where we went, not to the sea but the shore. I don't recall ever hearing the word "ocean" until I studied the geography, and history, of our situation, perhaps when I was eight or nine, already deep into a public school system that was as shallow as could be.

Columbus, I learned, sailed the Atlantic, hoping to find India. But he veered south and arrived in the Indies, wherever that was. South of here, south of Amboy. He came from Spain, where the priests burned Jews at the stake, from the same direction from which my mother's father fled in his youth, to arrive in New Jersey to marry a sixteen-year-old dark-eyed beauty whose own father had fled from that same direction a generation before. They made Jersey their home and never looked back, though they spoke in the parlance of their origins (though over the years less and less) until by the time I was listening they used Yiddish phrases more as punctuation to American English than as actual dialogue.

Stand at the Jersey shore, look straight ahead, and you might catch an imaginary glimpse of where most of my family had come from, the rough old regions of Eastern Europe and the even farther distant eastern ranges of old Russia. Except for my father, everyone I knew, adults, and friends my own age, had come, in ancestral boats and ships, from that direction. Ocean passages gave birth to clans, neighborhoods, Jersey towns.

Oh, Jersey shore! I stood there many an hour, looking east over the tops of the waves to the spuming horizon line where the ocean meets the sky, looking even farther east. I felt called, no doubt, still living out the story of my mother's side of the family. When I graduated from college I sailed to France, arriving at Le Havre on a beautiful summer morning, with the rising sun reflected in a thousand windows of the houses lined up beyond the port. I traveled farther east, well, at least as far east as Germany. But I discovered that Spain called out to me more, because of the Hemingway and company I had read, than the hometown kitchen-table stories about my ancestry, on my father's side, in western Russia and the steppes of the Russian east.

Our judgments, and our deepest affections for or spite for particular places, have to do with visceral events. Mine in relation to the Jersey shore were not pleasant, mostly a succession of summers that made for terrible sunburns. I'd walk down to the beach with my parents and brother, dive in and out of the endless succession of waves, sometimes swimming a ways out toward the pale blue horizon, feeling minor tides tugging at my legs, and then I'd swim back in what years later I realized was an intuitive (and rather pathetic) version of West Coast bodysurfing. I don't recall seeing any ships on that horizon. Those old beaches were endless flat strips of sand, as though this side of the country had been sheared down over the millennia by some giant handyman's plane. We lived at sea-level lives.

As I entered my adolescence, I spent a miserable string of summer nights at a rowdy Bradley Beach teenage hangout called Mike and Lou's, where year after year I plunged into deep crowds of Jersey kids and came up empty, alone, forlorn. If I had been a fisherman I would have starved to death early on.

At the end of those evenings I'd return to the rental rooms a few blocks from the beach that my parents dutifully reserved summer after summer, undressed, and lay on my bed, feeling as though from a mix of the heat from the sunburn and my unrequited desire for a girl, some girl, any girl, I was glowing in the dark. Too uncomfortable to sleep, I tried to read, using a flashlight while my younger brother slept on a cot next to my bed.

Did I read about Jersey? I wish I had. My fellow Jersey-ite Philip Roth years later wrote glowingly about this part of the coast in an essay he calls "Recollections Beyond the Last Rope." But long before that, the Jersey shore had a past in poetry. Our first American poet, Philip Freneau, grew up in Monmouth County, bordering on the ocean. The Atlantic served as the subject and occasion in the work of a number of great American poets after that, from Whitman to Frost to Elizabeth Bishop, and Hart Crane, and Wallace Stevens. On my four trans-Atlantic crossings (the first of which led to that vision of Le Havre and its windows reflecting the first sunlight of morning), I stood on the deck and looked out over the boundless wavescape, hypnotized by the horizon of endless variation within a form.

Nothing barred me from my watch. The Atlantic became for me an ocean on which to meditate on my past. Hart Crane celebrates that mood in his Caribbean seascapes, as in the middle stanzas of "Voyages II" in which he celebrates the sea "whose diapason knells / On scrolls of silver snowy sentences" and sings of "Adagios of islands…"

Adagios of islands! The Keys made lustrous by Wallace Stevens. Caribbean islets! Hart, Hart! For years my friends and I—boys who had never traveled farther west than Cleveland—dwelled on, quoted, chanted out loud and in our minds, lines from the last stanzas of "Voyages II" as though they were holy scripture: *"Bind us in time, O Seasons clear, and awe. / O minstrel galleons of Carib fire…"*

But there was another watch to keep, of which I was not yet aware, though the second hand and the minute hand and the hour hand kept moving, another sort of augury, one that Walt Whitman, long, long before I ever opened my eyes, had caught a glimpse of, without even ever having traveled anywhere near that destination.

"Facing west from California's shores," Whitman wrote...

> *Inquiring, tireless, seeking what is yet unfound,*
> *I, a child, very old, over waves, towards the house of maternity,*
> *The land of migrations, look afar,*
> *Look off the shores of my Western sea, the circle almost circled;*
> *For starting westward from Hindustan, from the vales of Kashmere,*
> *From Asia, from the north, from the God, the sage, and the hero,*
> *From the south, from the flowery peninsulas and the spice islands,*
> *Long having wander'd since, round the earth having wander'd,*
> *Now I face home again, very pleas'd and joyous,*
> *(But where is what I started for so long ago?*
> *And why is it yet unfound?)*

Many Eastern years went by before I turned my own face westward, and spent part of a winter in northern California, in an old Portuguese American fishing boat town turned university haven, arriving at night in San Francisco and traveling in the dark and fog over the nearby Santa Cruz Mountains on Highway 17 and finding, in the early morning, that only patches of fog remained, behind which unfurled that massive body of water, the Pacific, this ocean, home to whales and sharks and pilot fish and a billion other undersea creatures, the ocean celebrated by Keats who imagined the conquistadors staring at the Pacific for the first time and looking at each other "with a wild surmise—Silent, upon a peak in Darien..."

I felt as though I were standing on that same peak! The jagged, rocky northern California coast, the ocean extending out to the horizon like cool beaten pewter under a high morning sun, glowed in striking contrast with the flat and humid beach-lands of the East. Standing on the beach, I looked west, toward the Hawaiian

Islands, imagining that when the fog cleared I might see all the way to Indonesia and Japan and China. From a vaster distance than the Atlantic, great waves rolled toward me. Even at early morning some venturesome boys from town rode those swells on boards, styled, I learned much later, after those ridden by Hawaiian kings.

This is the ocean that Robinson Jeffers saw outside the window of his tower in Carmel and paid tribute to in "Continent's End," in which he feels behind him "Mountain and plain, the immense breadth of the continent" and before him "the mass and doubled stretch of water..."

This majestic ocean, unfurled, yes, unscrolling, rolling, rocking, heaving, crashing in constant falling back upon itself even in the farthest reaches I could see out beyond the breakers all the way to the horizon, this was a sea, this was not bound by Europe's western shores, or the British Isles, or western Africa, no, this was more than a navigable body of water, this was a vision, as in the great nineteenth-century European Romantics' notion of the sea as an image of the unbounded human imagination, with all its tidal sweep and currents and limitless possibilities. This is Melville's ocean that "rolls the midmost waters of the world, the Indian ocean and the Atlantic being but its arms. The same waves wash the moles of the new-built California towns, but yesterday planted by the recentest race of men, and lave the faded but still gorgeous skirts of Asiatic lands, older than Abraham; while all between float milk-ways of coral isles, and low-lying, endless, unknown archipelagoes, and impenetrable Japans. Thus this mysterious, divine Pacific zones the world's whole bulk about; makes all coasts one bay to it; seems the tide-beating heart of earth..."

It's not just a different watery vista you observe when standing on the California coast. When you look to the left and the right, north and south, and just a valley or two behind you, you find a different America than the one you notice in the East. Our home state of New Jersey owned a crazy-quilt pattern of Wasps and Irish Americans and Italian Americans and Polish Americans and some Jews and Dutch and even a touch here and there, more so now than when I was growing up, of some South Americans and Puerto Ricans and Carib islanders, all of these groups in counterpoint to the large minority of black folk, descendants of descendants of slaves, unwilling immigrants compared to the parents and grandparents and great-grandparents and so on of the rest of us. Most of our ancestors sailed the Atlantic to arrive on the eastern U.S. shores. Even in the second generation many of these so-called hyphenated Americans looked back, as I had, to the countries of their origins.

But here on the western edge of the continent, or the eastern edge of the Pacific, people looked different and looked at each other differently. This was still America, with its wild ethnic mixes, but you look around and see the evidence that you have traveled thousands of miles to a new location, and that the country has traveled in time. The California mix is different from the mix of the East, adding a Pacific swell to our already marvelous mélange of peoples: Mexicans and Malays, Tahitians and Vancouverites, French and Russian and Mandarin sounded on the air, Chinese and Hawaiians, Japanese and Okies, Salvadorians and Sumatrans, ex–New Yorkers and ex-Alabamians and ex-Polynesians, it was a Whitmanian mix, and only the great late poet could celebrate its oceanic fusion of colors, body types, languages, voices, literatures, cultures. (In the East, we had a melting pot. Here in California the demographic landscape seemed more an amalgam. From the design of houses and the tilt of neighborhoods to the food on the tables up and down the coast, life seemed more a fusion of presences than a melting away of differences.)

To this rocky coast my father had come, after a stopover in Hawaii in the late 1930s, putting his Old World behind him. Our west was his east. Before he ever saw the Atlantic, he crossed the Pacific. As a Red Air Force pilot on a training flight he had crashed his fighter plane in the Sea of Japan, spent time in China, and then sailed the Pacific to reach Hawaii and then San Francisco before entraining for the East Coast. There he flew tourist planes around Manhattan Island and met my mother at a dance in Brooklyn. Arriving here many decades later, I felt as though I were putting some of my own Old World behind.

"Hawaii was paradise," I remember him once saying, though he always spoke more about his time in Japan and China than of his trans-Pacific voyage. "I stayed there a number of days." Of San Francisco he said little, except that he found it to be a beautiful city, reminiscent in its colors of parts of Leningrad. When I think of him now, and the waters he sailed, it comes to me that the Atlantic has been my mother ocean and the Pacific a sign for my father and his trans-world-wanderings. If I can speak of myself in terms of those waters—and why not, since it makes sense now that I write about what those bodies of water have evoked in me?—I can say, though it has taken all these years for me to see this clearly, that I am Atlantic-born and my mother's child, but Pacific-bound, and my father's man.

Although for reasons of commerce and affection, I would choose—or was forced by circumstances to elect—to live in the East for a good part of every year, this coast, so new to me thirty years ago, and still new to me every day that I breathe the air and watch the ocean roll and break against the rocks above which I stand, welcomes me each time I arrive. I don't know how many others have come to this turn, how many others feel as I do about this matter. Perhaps demographics will show that what I take to be a merely personal decision will reveal a trend. Or not. I want to say that I can only speak for myself, but when I turn to the watery pages of *Moby-Dick*, I find once again that Melville speaks for me when he writes, "To any meditative Magian rover, this serene Pacific, once beheld, must ever be the sea of his adoption…"

I accept. Oh, Atlantic, waters near my home, though I will never forget you, it is over between us and has been a good long while! Pacific, with your waves, your swells, your roar, your air, your light, I am yours!

Originally published in the Antioch Review

ABOUT THE AUTHOR

Alan Cheuse is the author of the novels *The Bohemians* (1982), *The Grandmothers' Club* (1986), *The Light Possessed* (1990), and *To Catch the Lightning* (2008), the short fiction collections *Candace and Other Stories* (1980), *The Tennessee Waltz* (1991), and *Lost and Old Rivers* (1998), a pair of novellas published together as *The Fires* (2007), as well as the nonfiction work *Fall Out of Heaven: An Autobiographical Journey* (1987). As a book

Josh Cheuse

commentator, Cheuse is a regular contributor to National Public Radio's *All Things Considered*. He has edited with Caroline Marshall a volume of short stories, *Listening to Ourselves* (1994), and with Nicholas Delbanco, *Talking Horse: Bernard Malamud on Life and Work* (1997). He is also the editor of *Seeing Ourselves: Great Early American Short Stories* (2007) and coeditor, with Lisa Alvarez, of *Writers Workshop in a Book: The Squaw Valley Community of Writers on the Art of Fiction* (2007). His short fiction has appeared in publications such as the *New Yorker*, *Ploughshares*, the *Southern Review*, *Another Chicago Magazine*, and elsewhere.